Insiders and Outliers

Insiders and Outliers

The Individual in History

Gordon Wright

Stanford University

W. H. Freeman and Company
San Francisco

This book was published originally as a
part of *The Portable Stanford*, a series of
books published by the Stanford
Alumni Association, Stanford,
California, under the title *Insiders and
Outliers: A Procession of Frenchmen.*

Library of Congress Cataloging in Publication Data

Wright, Gordon, 1912–
 Insiders and outliers.

 Bibliography: p.
 Includes index.
 1. France—History—Addresses, essays, lectures.
I. Title.
DC110.W73 1981   944   81–9883
ISBN 0–7167–1339–X
ISBN 0–7167–1340–3 (pbk.)

Printed in the United States of America

1 2 3 4 5 6 7 8 9

For
Eric, Michael,
Philip, and David

. . . Why, 'tis a happy thing
To be a father unto many sons.
(Shakespeare, *King Henry the Sixth*)

CONTENTS

PREFACE

BOOKS, LIKE CHILDREN, are not always products of rational planning. This one is a case in point. Most of these essays were originally designed to be lectures, or were begun with no further object in mind than to satisfy my own curiosity. Most of them were in fact presented as lectures on various university campuses; and they would normally have suffered the customary fate of the lecture that dissolves into thin air (leaving at most a trace of verbal smog) as the last member of the audience departs. The idea of collecting them in book form emerged when Cyntha Fry Gunn, editor of the Stanford Alumni Association's "Portable Stanford" series, invited me to contribute a volume to that series. I am grateful to her and to Mr. John H. Staples of W. H. Freeman and Company for their joint belief that the essays might attract a wider audience.

The central theme that ties the book together—beyond the fact that it deals with a series of interesting but quite disparate Frenchmen—may not be obvious at first glance. It will emerge, I hope, from the introduction and the epilogue, in which I have expressed some of my ideas or prejudices about the nature and purpose of history. I do not take the view that history has a single message or meaning, or that only one sort of history is worth doing. History is a protean subject, partaking of both science and art, and all of its varied forms have something to contribute to our understanding. One of those forms is the study of individual human beings—especially as they respond to conditions of stress and crisis. It is the variety of human responses, and the ambiguities that dwell within human choices, that I find fascinating, and that probably come closest to providing a pervasive theme in the essays that follow.

Paris, April 1981   *Gordon Wright*

Insiders and Outliers

Myself: Portrait-Landscape by Henri Rousseau.

INTRODUCTION

Does the Individual Have a Place in History?

AN OXFORD DON OF ANCIENT VINTAGE, asked to explain his life-time love affair with the study of history, is supposed to have answered: "Why, because it's about chaps." This book is "about chaps" (or, since the characters are French, perhaps one should say it's about *mecs*). It may therefore strike some readers—especially those who follow what historians are writing these days—as either intentionally perverse, or as evidence that its author belongs to the Rip van Winkle school of historians. For a generation now, a kind of tidal wave has been carrying the new social historians to the forefront of the profession; and the members of that school, having tamed the computer to the point of riding it bareback, show little patience with those old-fashioned predecessors who focus on individual men or events. We now know, says eminent French social historian Fernand Braudel, that in fact the individual's role, past or present, is insignificant at best: he is "imprisoned within a destiny in which he himself has little free action, fixed in a landscape in which the infinite perspectives of the centuries stretch into the distance both behind him and before."

Viewed from this angle, individual men and women virtually

fade out of the picture. The record of the past becomes a record of economic and social forces, of trends and classes and demographic curves, until it ends (as the British sociologist Tom Bottomore puts it) in "a ghostly dance of bloodless categories." The new and fashionable school called the structuralists (most of whom are not historians but anthropologists, linguists, and literary critics) goes still further: its spokesmen find little difference between "primitive" and "advanced" cultures and see little change in the basic structures of human societies over time; for them, not only the individual but history itself ought to be consigned to the scrap heap. As for the most influential group of new social historians, the so-called *Annalistes* (from the title of their periodical *Annales: Economies, Sociétés, Civilisations),* the enemy to be destroyed is what they call *l'histoire événementielle:* i.e., "episodic" or "eventish" history, with its stress on politics and the state, on precise and dated events, on individual actions. "Eventish history," laments one rising star of the new generation, Michel Winock, "has been dying for an unconscionably long time." For him and for many of his contemporaries, it is something of a public scandal that the old-guard historians refuse to face facts and to admit that they're dead. Since the death notices have been posted, they might at the very least have the common decency to lie down.

It is not at all my purpose to issue a countermanifesto or to pick a fight with the new social historians. Indeed, I like to think (wishfully, perhaps?) that some of my best friends are social historians, and I am fully persuaded that they have brought a great deal of variety and excitement into our sometimes rather stodgy profession. They have been burrowing into some important questions that had long been neglected (partly because they were too complex or time-consuming in the precomputer age), and they have forced us to think beyond individuals and events into basic trends and structures. I am quite prepared to say, more power to them; even, perhaps, to echo the television commercial: "Thanks. We needed that!" More power to them—up to a point, anyway. But up to what point?

In my view, up to the point where the new social historians (some of them, at least) proclaim their intention to turn history into a rigorously predictive social science. Up to the point where they rule out uncertainty, refusing to consider alternative versions of the past ("what might have happened if . . .") or of the future. Up to the point where they brush aside as irrelevant the *ir*regularities and the exceptions in history. And up to the point where they rule out the play of the contingent and the unforeseen—the distorting impact of certain "chance" events and, yes, even of certain exceptional individuals.

The noted British historian Sir Alan Bullock, best known for his superb biography *Hitler: A Study in Tyranny,* has recently responded with unusual cogency to the challenge of the *sozialseientisch* historians. In a lecture at Cambridge in 1976, he replied to those who would try to make history "a kind of event-free social science, the task of which is to discover the norms of human behavior." He rejected the thesis that discrete events and individual actions are merely superficial happenings, distracting us from the far more important substratum of fundamental forces and trends that is both decisive and beyond human control. Drawing on his own special expertise in contemporary history, Bullock pointed to examples of decisive actions by certain individuals or small organized groups: Lenin in 1917, the German General Staff in 1916–18, the Zionist movement, Ataturk, Gandhi, Hitler, Mao, Castro. In each case basic forces and trends were operating, to be sure; but those forces did not dictate such outcomes as Bolshevik control of Russia, or Allied victory in 1918, or Soviet domination of Eastern Europe, or the Middle Eastern imbroglio produced by the creation of the state of Israel. "There are many ways of looking at human experience," Bullock concludes, "but there is still, I believe, room for one which . . . points to the gaps in the web of circumstance, the extent to which events confound the prophets, and the extent to which men . . . have contributed to making their own history."

No one is likely to make a more balanced or effective case for "eventish" history than Sir Alan Bullock. All that he asks, in fact, is equal time. Old-school historians in most cases stressed politics and the state, individuals and events, to the flagrant neglect of social and economic factors; the new social historians, he suggests, seem inclined to repeat the error of their predecessors in reverse. A blend of the two approaches to the past is, in his judgment, likely to give us the fullest and the richest context for understanding the past and using it for present purposes. In that blend the role of the individual actor and the play of the contingent and the unforeseen must once more be given their place.

One problem remains. Bullock's argument makes room for the truly exceptional individual whose actions at crucial moments may be decisive: the Lenins, the Hitlers, the Gandhis. But what of those individuals who were in no position to shape events, to throw the switches that send the historical train down a different track, or who had the opportunity but botched the job? Do they have a place in history? Some of the characters who will turn up in this book—most of them, in fact—belong to that less-exalted category. They were not extraordinary, nor were they so run-of-the-mill as to represent the typical citizen of their time. How am I to justify their inclusion in this procession of Frenchmen?

A few years ago, when I was seeking some rudimentary knowledge of the use of computers by the historian, a remark by a computer technician gave me pause. The technician displayed a neat graph (derived, I believe, from a sample of colonial North Carolina farmers) on which the data clustered in such a way as to produce a curve from which one could generalize. But out in left field so to speak were a number of lonely and isolated dots, representing individual farmers who didn't fit the pattern. "If I had my way," declared the expert with some exasperation, "all those outliers would simply go into the wastebasket."

I could understand the technician's exasperation: he was after norms and generalizations and laws, and the outliers simply confused the issue. Still there they were, and I could not help thinking that Hitler, Lenin, Gandhi would no doubt have shown up on a graph as outliers. So too would a goodly number of lesser figures out of the past; yet they existed, and contributed something to the kaleidoscopic variety of their times. Perhaps their role, as sociologist Emile Durkheim suggested, was to make it easier for the society to define the current limits of normality and acceptability. And in some cases—notably in times of upheaval, rapid change, or severe social stress—they may have emerged from obscurity for a time, spinning in the whirlpools and eddies of events before being sucked under once more.

The title of this book promises some attention to insiders as well as outliers—figures, that is, who belong in the mainstream or can claim membership in a power elite of sorts. Surely a Lamartine, a Clemenceau or a Jaurès, and above all a Charles de Gaulle would have to be classed as insiders, as part of the Establishment. Yet even these men diverge from the norm in obvious and important ways. They are clearly individuals, not typical representatives of some category or class. They demonstrate, in other words, that even insiders can sometimes be outliers. Indeed, that may be what makes them especially intriguing.

Confession is said to be good for the soul. I may as well confess, then, that I have always had a persistent curiosity about outliers—an urge to delve into their backgrounds, to discover what made them different from the normal run, and what they did when chance, fate, or deep underlying forces offered them some kind of opportunity to break the surface. This is not what historians, if they are serious, are supposed to do. We are reputed to be an austere and bloodless lot, immune to the temptations of the colorful and adventurous sides of life around us, whether past or present. Yet occasionally, with appropriate misgivings, some of us allow ourselves to be drawn into the pursuit of an intriguing facet of the past— a person, an episode—that attracts us in part because it piques our curiosity or tickles our fancy. Then we suspend our weighty reflection for a few hours and embark on the equivalent of a busman's holiday, digging about in dusty corners of the archives for no other reason than the sheer pleasure of it. In part, this book reflects such a nonconformist impulse. I hope that some readers may find pleasure in it too. And that they may even find, buried here and there, a provocative idea or two.

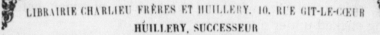

Frontispiece from *Mémoires de Vidocq*.

1

Two Adventurers
in an Age of Crisis: or,
Balzac for Real

ONE CAN HARDLY ARGUE that Gabriel Ouvrard and Eugène Vidocq belong to Hegel's category of "world-historical figures" who shaped or deflected the course of human history. Nor can one argue that they were so ordinary as to typify their age— to embody the traits of the silent majority in Revolutionary and post-Revolutionary France. Indeed, in their different ways they stand out as quite atypical: as perfect examples of those outliers who stubbornly remain strangers to any statistical curve. Yet in their very eccentricity one can see an important aspect of an age of revolution: its tendency to scramble the social system, and to bring into positions of prominence and power men who in ordinary times might never have emerged from the shadows.

The lives of the two men in question ran parallel for a half century, intersecting at times and then diverging again. Both of them flashed across the sky like shooting stars: both briefly became celebrities, even legends; yet both died in obscurity and were quickly forgotten. One of them has sometimes been called "the Napoleon of Finance"; the other, "the Napoleon of the Police." One of them (and possibly both) directly inspired Balzac's pen, as well as those of Victor Hugo, Eugène Sue, and other lesser literary lights. One of them (perhaps both) achieved immortality not in history books or in the memories of his countrymen but in the pages of great novels, concealed under such fictional names as Jean Valjean, Javert, Vautrin, Baron de Nucingen.

Both men were true Balzacian figures, out of that complex Parisian world that Balzac created from a blend of reality and his own fertile imagination. During Balzac's lifetime (1799–1850), France was being transformed from a rural agrarian nation into a semimodern industrial and urbanized society. Young provincials flocked to Paris, drawn by the promise of wealth and power and undeterred by the risks of disasters. The age was eminently suited to the strong, the venturesome, the unscrupulous. Balzac, himself one of the young provincials on the make, set out to delineate in almost infinite detail the life and society of his time. His vast fresco called The Human Comedy, made up of almost a hundred interconnected novels, focused mainly on the bourgeoisie—that aggressive, energetic, ruthless stratum whose leaders were rapidly displacing the old aristocracy in the years after Napoleon's fall. Frenchmen from that day until our own time have absorbed their knowledge of the period from Balzac rather than from the historians. A poll in 1978 found more Frenchmen reading Balzac than any other author, even the most eminent moderns.

Balzac's world was one that also fascinated one of his contemporaries, Karl Marx. It was Marx's ambition to write a book about Balzac, if and when he finished his own work on what Marx himself impatiently called "this economic s---." Friedrich Engels, Marx's alter ego, wrote that he had "learned more from Balzac than from all the historians, economists, and statisticians put together." As for Balzac himself, he made no bones about borrowing great chunks of reality as he sought to catch the spirit of bourgeois life in the Paris of his day. Indeed, he remarked at one point that the novelist must constantly guard

Detail from a view of the Place de la Concorde in Balzac's time by Guiseppe Canella.

against spoiling "the true by seemingly dramatic devices, especially when real life itself assumes the form of fiction." The Paris of his time, he said, was filled with "capricious tangles of coincidence" that far outstripped the contrivances of the imagination. Indeed, he added, reality was sometimes so excessive that the novelist dared not use it raw: he must first "tone it down, purify and chasten it" in order to be believed.

Both Gabriel Ouvrard and Eugène Vidocq came of age during that vast upheaval called by the French *the* Revolution (to distinguish it from all the lesser ones to follow). A decadent monarchy, heavily in debt from past extravagance and confronted by rising challenges from the old aristocracy and the new bourgeoisie, opened the flood gates by convening an Estates-General in 1789. For the next generation, Frenchmen were to live in a state of chronic crisis, as moderate reformers challenged royal authority only to be outflanked by a series of more radical factions. Eventually, after the excesses of Jacobin dictatorship and the Reign of Terror, came a pause and an almost inevitable period of reaction, to be followed by an era of authoritarian rule under Napoleon Bonaparte. Such times offered opportunity, and also danger.

Gabriel Ouvrard was born in western France (the Vendée region) in 1770; Eugène Vidocq in the northeast, near the Belgian border, in 1775. Both were of relatively humble bourgeois origin: the senior Ouvrard owned a small paper mill, Vidocq's father a corner bakery. But fate, during their adolescent years, dealt them quite different hands.

Ouvrard's father sent him off at age eighteen to make his way in the nearest city, Nantes, where young Gabriel was apprenticed to a wholesale grocer. He was quickly saved from that drab fate by the Revolutionary events of 1789. In Versailles, the Estates-General converted itself into a National Assembly and, with the help of the increasingly vocal Paris crowd (which attacked and took the Bastille and otherwise made its influence felt), drafted a constitution and proclaimed a new era. Sensing that the upheaval in Paris would create a vast new market for newsprint, Ouvrard bought up on credit the next two years' output of all the paper mills in the west. From this venture he made a modest killing, whereupon he saw before him an even greater opportunity: the prospect of runaway inflation and a severe food crisis. With his initial profits he set up shop as a food wholesaler, specializing in imported colonial goods from the West Indies. By 1793 he was reputed to be the youngest millionaire in Nantes.

From Paris, however, came an ominous new threat. In 1793 an emergency government headed by Maximilien Robespierre and supported by the network of the Jacobin clubs throughout France took on the traits of a modern totalitarian regime. In its determination to purge the new republic of bad citizens, and to fuel public enthusiasm for the war against an enemy coalition, the government decreed judicial shortcuts and embarked on a Reign of Terror. Accused by the Jacobins of profiteering at the people's expense, Ouvrard avoided arrest, though just barely, thanks to influential contacts plus some fast footwork on his own part. When Robespierre was overthrown in 1794 and the Terror wound down, Ouvrard could at last draw an easy breath and could think about greater worlds to conquer. He set forth for Paris, loaded with francs and with dreams of business adventure.

Young Vidocq, meanwhile, was finding the ladder of success a good deal more slippery. From early childhood he had all the makings of a successful juvenile delinquent: he was hot tempered, pugnacious, incorrigible. His father apprenticed him to a baker, but the job bored him beyond measure. He spent hours hanging about the local barracks, where the soldiers taught him swordplay. By age fifteen, he later claimed, he had killed two men in duels. He was equally precocious as a womanizer: a handsome, passionate blond, he cut a wide swath among the women of the town (and continued his successes until the very end, at age eighty-two).

Early on, he took to pilfering from his father's cash drawer, despite scoldings and threats. At last, restless for adventure, he broke open the parental strongbox and cleaned out the contents, with which he set off for the coast to take ship to

America. On the way, however, he fell in with bad companions who robbed him of all he had; and at age sixteen, he enlisted in the Revolutionary army. With just a bit more self-discipline he might have worked his way up to a marshal's baton in Napoleon's army; others did so, and Vidocq clearly had the requisite talent. But his rambunctious temper betrayed him. Between occasional battles, he fought a long series of duels, engaged in brief and torrid love affairs, and at last was cashiered from the army after challenging his entire regiment to fight him one after another. He drifted for a time from one obscure adventure to the next, and finally turned up once more at home, where he was greeted as the prodigal son by his permissive parents. They promptly found him a bride with a dowry, and helped set up the couple in a corner grocery.

Insufferable boredom set in almost at once. Vidocq set off again on a series of rolling-stone adventures that included, he later recalled, a spell as a circus roustabout and a period of shanghaied service in the Dutch navy. His rowdy habits now began to catch up with him. After one of his customary fights over a woman, he was jailed for the first (but not the last) time. Bad luck led to worse: he was shortly charged with forging a legal document designed to get one of his cellmates out of prison; for this offense, he was sentenced in 1796 to eight years at hard labor in the galleys. In fact, Vidocq always insisted that he had been framed by his fellow prisoners, and that his first condemnation, by an ironic quirk of fate, was for one of the few sins he had never committed. Off he went, then, to the galleys or *bagne* at Brest, where the most hardened criminals served their time, chained at night to wooden benches on old hulks docked at a naval base, and did heavy labor on shore during the day. It was a sad prospect for a handsome, restless young man of twenty-one.

Ouvrard meanwhile was riding high in the Paris of the Directory (1795–99). The new regime, headed by an executive committee of five directors represented a pendulum swing away from the grim and rigid fanaticism of the Jacobin era. It was a time of runaway inflation, of endless war, of relaxed ethical standards—a time of infinite possibilities for a clever opportunist with a bit of a bankroll and a taste for risk. Ouvrard set up shop as a private banker and entrepreneur. He soon talked his way into close contact with the inner circles of government and landed a lucrative contract as supplier to both the French navy and the allied Spanish navy. On the side, he provided loans at handsome interest to the government itself, which kept going in that era by hand-to-mouth methods. Before long, though still a stripling in his late twenties, he was one of the richest and most powerful figures of Paris society. He bought up town houses and chateaux wholesale; he staged parties that were the talk of Paris; he acquired as his mistress the notorious Madame Tallien, reputed to be the most beautiful (and most expensive) woman in town. Gossip had it that the venal Director Barras had persuaded Ouvrard, in return for governmental favors, to take over Madame Tallien from Barras himself, who was finding the lady too costly for his budget.

Then came disaster. In late 1799 a young Corsican general swept the Directory out of existence, and with it all of Ouvrard's high governmental contacts. For Ouvrard, one government was like another. He declared himself ready to do business with the new regime but found the regime unreceptive. To First Consul Napoleon Bonaparte, all bankers and army suppliers were swindlers, "the scourge and scum of nations," concerned only to make a quick franc. A bitter squabble ensued; on Bonaparte's orders, Ouvrard's naval supply contract was canceled, and his effort to recover the ten million francs he had loaned to the Directory met a blunt refusal. Still, Ouvrard kept his temper and played for time. He sensed that Napoleon could not manage to govern France and pursue his wars without the help of an expert who could provide funds and equip his armies. Before long Napoleon swallowed his pride and called on Ouvrard for help. The young financier found himself entrusted with a whole series of tasks—supplying the army, feeding the hungry cities, and building a fleet of transports for the coming invasion of England. All this he agreed to do without any appropriation of government funds. He raised the money on his personal credit, on the assumption that he would be handsomely repaid later by the grateful

Madame Tallien by Louis-Gabriel-Eugène Isabey.

Bonaparte. He borrowed; he mortgaged; he sold most of his chateaux and town houses. His indebtedness reached the astronomical figure of sixty-seven million francs. Never, though, did he lose his confidence or his nerve; he was always ready with another ingenious scheme to recoup his fortunes.

When Napoleon brusquely abandoned his plan to invade England and set off overland to fight in central Europe, Ouvrard approached the minister of finance with his newest scheme. Aware that the government's coffers were empty, Ouvrard offered to provide the treasury with still another large loan, in return for which he asked only that all tax revenues for the next several years be assigned to him. The hard-pressed minister signed, and in addition agreed to send Ouvrard to Madrid with a mission to collect a large sum owed to France by the Spanish government. Ouvrard's plan of operations was dazzlingly simple. The Spanish treasury, like that of France, was chronically empty; but off in Mexico, vast piles of silver bullion had been piling up for some years, immobilized there by the British sea blockade. If this asset could be unfrozen somehow, Ouvrard might save everybody's skin—his own, as well as that of the Spanish and the French governments.

The Madrid mission prospered; as always, Ouvrard was a persuasive salesman of ideas. His proposal, welcomed by the Spanish king, involved a complex arrangement with Europe's biggest banking house, Hope of Amsterdam. For a commission, Hope would arrange to trade the Mexican silver for American cotton, tobacco, and sugar, which would then be conveyed through the British blockade in American ships to neutral ports in Europe. Everything seemed ready to go, when calamity struck once more. Napoleon, now elevated from first consul to emperor, came storming back to Paris in 1805 after his great victory at Austerlitz to find the treasury empty, the Spanish contribution to his war still unpaid, and tax receipts for several future years signed over to Ouvrard.

At a meeting with his ministers, Napoleon threw a tantrum such as only he could throw: he raged for hours, fulminating against the unfortunate finance minister and threatening to hang Ouvrard on a gallows so high that everybody in France could see the execution. All government obligations to Ouvrard were canceled, and he was ordered by the emperor to pay the state one hundred forty million francs to boot—or face imprisonment. This time there was no escape. Ouvrard sold off most of his remaining property, turned over the costly asset Madame Tallien to a new husband, and finally in 1807 was forced to declare bankruptcy. His private creditors now came swarming about, and they soon had him committed to Sainte-Pélagie, the debtors' prison in Paris. Within one short decade, the youthful financial genius had gone from riches to rags; his brilliant business career appeared to be in shambles.

At least Ouvrard's condition was no worse than Vidocq's: that young hothead was paying a harsh penalty for his impulsive follies. Condemned to the galleys in 1796, he was shipped off to Brest in a ritual later described in memorable prose in Victor Hugo's early novel *The Last Day of a Condemned Man*. Twice a year the condemned prisoners from northern France were assembled at Bicêtre prison near Paris, whence the convoys departed. As crowds of sensation seekers looked on, each convict was fitted with an iron collar and leg irons, by which he was chained to an open cart. Then the convoy set off on the long journey to Brest or Toulon, taunted and insulted by residents along the route, exposed day and night to sun and storm, until the exhausted felons reached their grim destination. For Vidocq, however, the stay at Brest lasted only a week. Somehow he got hold of sailor's clothing, managed to cut his chains, and talked his way past the night guards. He took to the road, moving on frequently from adventure to adventure. For a time he hired on as teacher in a village school, and at one point evaded detection by disguising himself as a nun. Recognized and arrested at last, he soon found himself back in the galleys again—this time at Toulon, and in double chains.

But Vidocq was obsessed by the idea of freedom, and made repeated attempts to escape. At last he succeeded, thanks to the help of a young woman of the region whose sympathies he had managed to arouse. Off he went again on his wanderings—several years this time of running before the law, in the fashion of Jean Valjean in Hugo's *Les Misérables*. Valjean's vicissitudes must surely have been copied from Vidocq's: Hugo's hero lived under the constant threat of exposure and was finally tracked down—after achieving wealth and status—by the human bloodhound Javert (also drawn from the protean model Vidocq!). The real Vidocq at each stage found an impressionable woman to take him in, but sooner or later he was recognized and blackmailed by some ex-convict from the *bagne* and was forced to move on. Tiring at last of this hunted existence, he made the decision that transformed his life: he went to the prefect of police in Paris and offered his services as informer, proposing to identify escaped convicts and criminal gangs that were plotting mischief. After considerable hesitation, the prefect decided to take the risk.

So in 1809, as the ex-tycoon Ouvrard found the doors of debtors' prison closing behind him, the ex-jailbird Vidocq's name was added to the police payroll. After so many vicissitudes, he had finally found his calling. He began as simple stool pigeon, placed in prison cells to eavesdrop on unwary inmates. Then he was allowed outside, entrusted with the task of infiltrating criminal gangs. At last, when his successful efforts had blown his cover, he persuaded the authorities to let him organize a special unit called the *Sûreté:* it consisted of a dozen handpicked men who had served their time in the galleys and who knew the underworld well. Before long, the *Sûreté* had achieved a remarkable reputation; some called it the most efficient police force anywhere in Europe. Its descendant, the *Sûreté Nationale,* continues to enjoy great prestige in France's police administration today.

Ouvrard meanwhile was pining away in debtors' prison. "Pining," however, might be too strong a word; his condition could have been worse. The French debtors' prison in those days was a curious institution, far less dismal than the ordinary jail. Technically, a debtor was not a condemned criminal. Any creditor could call on the courts to detain the debtor for a maximum of five years, or until he or his friends agreed to repay the debt. If the debtor had managed to conceal some of his resources and refused to pay up, he could draw on those hidden funds to live more or less comfortably while under detention. So it was with Ouvrard, who set himself up in style. He bought the use of the adjoining room from its occupant, and arranged a kind of two-room suite complete with comfortable furniture, rugs, and papered walls. For a time, he was said to have rented an apartment across the street where he installed cook and servants. Friends were invited to his quarters for dinner parties and musical evenings. Off and on Ouvrard spent four years here. He was finally released in 1813 on a plea of ill health, and without repaying a centime to his creditors. Better still, he was out just in time to see the downfall of his old nemesis, Napoleon.

The emperor had hastened his own downfall by his disastrous invasion of Russia in 1812. Hard pressed for troops to fend off the armies of the European coalition arrayed against him, he managed to hold on until the spring of 1814, but was then overwhelmed by numbers. Captured by the invaders, Napoleon was shipped off to exile on the island of Elba, and was replaced by the restored Bourbon pretender, Louis XVIII. A quarter century of upheaval had thus brought France full circle, back to the old monarchy.

In less than a year, however, Napoleon was back in power again. King Louis's regime quickly made itself unpopular, opening the way to the ex-emperor's dramatic escape from Elba and triumphal return to Paris. Ouvrard, who had no reason to love Napoleon, showed nevertheless that he held no grudges—at least when it came to business deals. When the restored emperor appealed to him for help, he responded with alacrity: once again he took on the task of supplying the French armies, and he accompanied Napoleon's forces as far as Waterloo. This time it was the emperor's last hurrah. Only a hundred days after his return from Elba Napoleon was once again a captive ex-emperor, and this time was exiled to the south Atlantic island of St. Helena. Ouvrard once more was out of a job, and in disgrace.

Irrepressible as always, Ouvrard now offered his services to the restored Bourbons, who kept him, understandably, at arm's length. But after a year or so the king's ministers began

Gabriel Julien Ouvrard by Henri Georges Villain.

to grow desperate. The treasury was weighed down by past indebtedness from Napoleon's wars and by the cost of maintaining allied occupation troops in France. To raise taxes would make the monarchy still more unpopular, and a government bond issue was sure to find few takers. So when Ouvrard approached the ministers once more with a solution, they listened.

His plan was imaginative and in advance of its time. He proposed to give France for the first time a stable fiscal system in place of the hand-to-mouth financing of the past. This would involve the creation of a long-term national debt and a sinking fund; a portion of the government's revenues would be channeled to the sinking fund, the interest from which would be used to reduce the national debt. The government, in order to restore confidence in its paper, would guarantee to repay all past and future debts; it would then arrange with the largest banks of Europe to float a large bond issue carrying generous interest. Investors all over Europe, declared Ouvrard, would leap at the chance to participate; the bonds would quickly shoot up in value, so that everyone—bondholders, banks, government—would gain.

The royal authorities hesitated for a time. The plan seemed too good to be true. But at last they adopted it, and things went as Ouvrard had predicted. The first issue was snapped up by British and Dutch investors, and soon Frenchmen as well were demanding a piece of the action. Bond values shot up; everyone did in fact win. Everyone, that is, except Ouvrard himself. His recompense was to have been the right to buy several millions of francs worth of bonds at the initial offering price. He neglected, however, to get that promise in writing, and the government officials subsequently denied that any such promise had been made. Ouvrard's greatest triumph thus ended in his greatest personal disappointment.

Nonetheless, the venture had at least restored his standing as a financial genius. He was back once again in the salons of the high society of Paris, so well established as to marry off his daughter to a ranking aristocrat. He lived well, in a town house located on the present site of the United States Embassy, and his business affairs prospered. In addition, a few years later he had a new opportunity to display his talent as organizer of army supply. A liberal revolution in Spain had forced King Ferdinand to accept a constitution, and this threatening precedent led the European powers in 1823 to delegate the French to be the restorers of law and order. The French armies headed south, but soon found themselves stalled by lack of adequate transport vehicles, horses, and food. Ouvrard offered his expertise on a cost-plus basis, and he delivered the goods. From that point onward, the armies rolled straight to Madrid without suffering a single shortage. Ouvrard's agents preceded the troops by one day, announcing that they would buy the peasants' produce at a good price: if delivered before 8:00 A.M., the price would be ten times the going rate. The system worked miraculously.

Arriving in Madrid, Ouvrard was as always bursting with ambitious schemes. The Spanish colonies in America had by now broken away, and Ouvrard set out to persuade King Ferdinand to join him in reconquering the lost territories. He proposed a partnership between Ferdinand and himself to set up a private company that would recruit its own army and would take over Spanish America, thenceforward monopolizing its trade for the advantage of the partners. The king showed serious interest, but before the deal could be concluded, Ouvrard was called back to Paris. The authorities there were pleased at the army's quick and easy triumph, but a number of leading politicians raged at the size of the bill presented by Ouvrard. Parliament set up an investigating committee, which cleared him of the charge of profiteering. But a cry of "whitewash!" went up in the press, impelling the prime minister to set up a royal commission to review the verdict. Its findings were disastrous for Ouvrard. He was denounced as an unscrupulous gouger, and his claim for payment rejected.

As though this were not enough, a second mishap added to his miseries. For a dozen years a onetime partner had been pursuing him in the courts over an alleged debt; in 1824 the court at last decided for the plaintiff and ordered Ouvrard to pay at once. Outraged, Ouvrard refused. He hid out, and for some weeks the police hunted him in vain. At last the aggrieved creditor persuaded a noted detective to take up the

Vidocq, poacher turned gamekeeper, making an arrest.

search; within days, Ouvrard was routed out of hiding and locked up once more in debtors' prison. The detective who performed so efficiently was, of course, Vidocq. It was the only time, apparently, that the paths of the two men crossed.

Vidocq during the preceding dozen years had been making himself into a legend: a mix, one might say, of Sherlock Holmes, James Bond, and Georges Simenon's Inspector Maigret. His small police unit, never consisting of more than twenty-five men, had remarkable success in rounding up criminal gangs both in Paris and in the surrounding region. Ex-convicts themselves, Vidocq's men were not always entirely scrupulous in their methods; they knew the Paris underworld and borrowed its tactics. Vidocq himself often operated single-handed and took on the most dangerous assignments. He was a master of disguise and of what later generations would call the quick draw; his assets included a cool brain and remarkable physical strength. No doubt some of the exploits attributed to him were apocryphal, but enough truth underlay the stories to justify the myth. One of the most spectacular coups occurred in 1819, when he and a few assistants captured a band of sixty cutthroats and thieves known as the *chauffeurs du Nord:* Vidocq prepared the way by infiltrating the gang and leading them into a trap. When at last he paid a visit to his natal town, which he had left in disgrace, he was lionized: the local boy had made good.

Success and notoriety, however, can breed trouble. Vidocq's contempt for the regular police bred anger and jealousy. There were reports of a police plot to have him assassinated, and the prefect for a time insisted—over Vidocq's protests—that he accept a bodyguard. The critics of his unorthodox methods finally put enough pressure on the prefect to force Vidocq's resignation as chief of the *Sûreté*. He retired in 1828 to a Parisian suburb, where he wrote his memoirs in three volumes—with considerable touching up by ghostwriters hired by his publisher. The work was an instant best-seller. Victor Hugo read it, and sat down at once to write his novelette *The Last Day of a Condemned Man*. Balzac met Vidocq at a dinner party and went away fascinated; soon thereafter, he introduced into one of his novels a new character, Vautrin, who was to reappear as a central figure in a half-dozen Balzacian tales. Eugène Sue, as he planned his pop classic *The Mysteries of Paris*, consulted Vidocq on underworld life and criminal argot.

A business venture, however, turned sour and cost Vidocq both his savings and his royalties. He had set up a small factory that employed only ex-convicts, thus combining philanthropy with business; he produced such items as counterfeit-proof paper and thief-proof locks. When the experiment failed (largely because he lacked business experience and talent), Vidocq went back to his true calling: he opened a private detective agency that soon boasted twelve thousand clients and a confidential file that J. Edgar Hoover might have envied. His position at last seemed stable, and his future assured.

Ouvrard during this time had been serving his second stretch in debtors' prison, interrupted for a period by transfer to a real prison (the Paris Conciergerie, where Marie Antoinette had been incarcerated during the Revolution) on charges stemming from the army supply episode. Even in the Conciergerie he managed to live in reasonable comfort; in both regular prisons and debtors' prisons, jailkeepers were permitted to rent out more commodious quarters to paying customers, so that Ouvrard could continue to do business and hold court in this unlikely headquarters. Like Vidocq, he used some of his enforced leisure to produce three volumes of memoirs. They were only modestly successful with the public, however; business deals lacked the glamour of crime and police work.

Ouvrard emerged from prison in 1829, brimming over as usual with energy and ideas. But though he failed to realize it, his days of fame and fortune were over. New banking firms, notably Rothschild, had moved up into control of the Paris financial world. They had less imagination than Ouvrard, but they had more cash and more connections and could effectively block his comeback. Ouvrard, angry and jealous, spent these Balzacian years vainly trying to recoup his fortunes and to humiliate the Rothschilds, mainly by playing the stock market in Paris and London. Occasionally he scored a success, but he was too impulsive and unsystematic to compete in the new business world; he kept getting into tangles that ended in the courts. He survived on the fringes of the big money; he was never destitute but remained an outsider. A reader of Balzac keeps expecting Ouvrard to turn up in some novel—and perhaps there is a touch of him in the Baron de Nucingen, the wealthy parvenu stock-market operator who appears in a half dozen of Balzac's romances.

When Ouvrard died in 1846, alone in his small London flat, the Paris newspapers carried long and somewhat romanticized accounts of his fabulous career. Here was a man who had repeatedly made and lost millions, who had circulated among the great figures of his age, yet who left behind no lasting memorial—no bank, no institution, no great idea. His favorite epigram, "Taxes kill, borrowing rejuvenates," reflects the spirit of the born entrepreneur. He was buried in the famed Paris cemetery of Père Lachaise, where at the end of *Père Goriot* Balzac's Rastignac, a young provincial out to make his fortune in the big city, looks out over the vast metropolis and cries: "Now, Paris, it's between you and me!"

During Ouvrard's last struggle to climb the greasy pole of success, Vidocq was prospering mightily in his new career as private detective. So mightily, indeed, that a fateful boomerang effect ensued. His success once again aroused the irritation and jealousy of the regular police. They berated him about his methods (as usual, not always orthodox); they infiltrated his staff with undercover agents; and at last, in 1842, they moved in on him by force. Several dozen policemen converged on his office, carted him off to jail, and combed through his files in search of irregularities. Since *habeas corpus* had (and has) no place in the French legal code, he was kept for seven months in solitary confinement while government prosecutors prepared the case against him. The court found him guilty of a long series of technical illegalities and condemned him to five years of prison plus a heavy fine. The verdict brought a furious outburst from the courtroom crowd, solidly on his side. It appeared that he might end his career as he began it—a long-term convict, the victim of the misplaced energies of the police and the courts, and perhaps of his own penchant for crime-busting through the use of the criminals' own methods.

From this fate he was saved, however, by a new and talented lawyer who appealed his case. In the courtroom, the attorney dramatically recounted Vidocq's colorful career, his notable achievements, and a long list of good deeds on behalf of the poor and miserable. Toward the end of his summation, the judge is said to have interrupted, crying: "Enough! Free this man at once!" Free he went, to the cheers of the crowd. Returning to his office, he found his staff gone, his invaluable files scattered. Old and dispirited, he sold out in 1847. Some have hinted that Alphonse de Lamartine, head of the provisional government during the revolution of 1848, used him in some sort of semiofficial police capacity, but the evidence for this is shaky. Vidocq dropped out of sight for several years, until the new emperor, Napoleon III, learned that he was living in poverty in the slums, and awarded him a small pension.

Although he was nearing eighty by then, Vidocq was still a powerful and impressive figure in his neighborhood. Some said that he had a series of younger mistresses, and made out wills in favor of each in turn. When he died in 1857, there were few left to mourn him or even to remember. A hundred people turned up at his funeral, most of them poor residents of the quarter whom he had befriended, along with his last true love, a beautiful young blonde. His place of burial has gone unrecorded. Like Ouvrard, he passed through history like a meteor, vanishing quickly from public memory. But unlike Ouvrard, Vidocq left a clearly identifiable image in the most representative novels of the time, plus a permanent monument in the form of the *Sûreté Nationale.*

Ouvrard and Vidocq may not have been typical of their times, nor even especially memorable for the mark they left on history. Yet their careers help bring to life the age in which they lived: an age of social upheaval and economic change that saw the rise of the bourgeoisie, scratching and clawing its way to the top of the social heap. And perhaps they were eccentrics in the Durkheimian sense—the kind of people who by their unorthodox behavior permit a society to define the boundaries of what is normal and acceptable. Both men, in a sense, straddled that boundary in the Balzacian age.

Historians of our day rarely find space to mention either Ouvrard or Vidocq, but there are occasional exceptions. The French scholar Louis Chevalier, seeking to catch the spirit of early nineteenth-century Paris, has this to say: "The legend of Vidocq, combining in one person . . . order and disorder, police and crime, dirty work and high politics, was an important element in popular thinking. The massive silhouette, now reassuring and now terrifying, not only loomed in the background of the major contemporary works, but also dominated popular fears and beliefs." And here is the Harvard historian David Landes on the Parisian financial world of Balzac's time: "When, every so often a maverick appeared, like this Ouvrard who spent his life doggedly fighting the stolid, conservative powers of French finance, opposing their wealth with his imagination, their influence with his energy and persuasiveness, their self-righteous complacency with his mercurial ambition, always falling only to rise again with some new idea . . . , then the ranks [of the business establishment] were closed and held. . . . A man . . . whose business morals were so weak that he not only competed with the Rothschilds, but attacked them in print, who embarrassed a colleague with truths and half-truths about his profits and thereby let the public into some of the secrets of the profession? There was room for newcomers, but not for rowdies."

Il est un secret qui me tue,
Que je dérobe aux regards curieux,
Vous ne voyez ici que la Statue,
L'âme se cache à tous les yeux.

22 Xbre 1835

Lacenai

Frontispiece from *Mémoires de Lacenaire*.

2

Two Unlikely Heroes: or, Murder as Art Form and Source of Literary Inspiration

THE ENGLISH WRITER THOMAS DE QUINCEY, best remembered for his *Confessions of an Opium Eater*, published in 1827 an essay entitled "Murder Considered as One of the Fine Arts." It purported to scold a group of fashionable young Londoners who had formed a "Society of Connoisseurs in Murder"; the members engaged in learned discussions of the latest in European homicides. The essay was plainly satirical in tone, and caused something of a scandal. Viewed in retrospect, we are told by the French philosopher-historian Michel Foucault, the essay called attention to a new literary phenomenon in early nineteenth-century England and France: the emergence of a genre of crime literature that glorified violent crime because, in Foucault's words, "it is one of the fine arts, because it can be committed only by exceptional individuals, because it reveals the monstrous nature of the rich and powerful." In this new genre, Foucault argues in his best-seller *Discipline and Punish,* "crime becomes the exclusive privilege of those who possess real greatness. Quality murders [*les beaux meurtres*] are not for the cheap-jack criminal."

Foucault advances a complex and ingenious explanation for this strange phenomenon and for the sharp contrast between this new crime literature and the popular variety (broadsheets, mainly) that preceded it in the seventeenth and eighteenth centuries. Put bluntly, his theory suggests that the older genre had permitted the common people to identify with the great criminals who were driven by want or injustice to break the law and who fully atoned for their transgressions by public torture, confession, and execution. The power elite, in an effort to rupture the dangerous emotional link between criminal and common man, abolished public torture and suppressed the broadsheets that had transmuted murderers into popular heroes. In the new genre of crime literature, Foucault contends, "the common people were robbed of their old pride in their crimes; the great murders became a quiet game played by the well behaved."

Except for Foucault's admirers and disciples (and there are many of these, both at home and abroad), his thesis may seem more ingenious than convincing. But the phenomenon he observes here would be hard to deny: there *was* a new variety of crime literature in the early decades of the nineteenth century, and some criminals found themselves objects of passionate public interest, lionized by a considerable sector of the social elite. Other social deviants, however, had to wait much longer to be rediscovered and lionized—in another era, and for other reasons. An example of each type may tell us something about that period, and perhaps about our own as well.

November 12, 1835: two young men stand in the dock of the French criminal courts—one in Paris, the other in Caen, the chief city of Normandy. Both defendants are of rural origin. Both are physically unimpressive, measuring in at scarcely more than five feet in height—though an abundant shock of black hair makes each seem taller. Both men freely confess their crimes and ask for speedy execution. Both are quickly found guilty (the trials lasting two and three days respectively) and are sentenced to die by the guillotine.

Both of these murderers are destined to become (though at different points in time) legendary figures, celebrated in popular and serious literature and even in those modern art forms, the cinema and television. One of them has been called "the Napoleon of crime" and "the first man to professionalize crime and to train for it." Of the other it has recently been said that "if the peasants had a Plutarch [to eulogize their great men], he would have his chapter in the *Illustrious Lives*." One of these two killers inspired a classic Russian novel, *Crime and Punishment;* the other was made the central figure of a film that in the mid-1970s achieved a kind of cult status in Paris. Yet the names of Pierre-François Lacenaire and Pierre Rivière rarely turn up in "serious" history books, and no doubt there is good reason for that neglect. Writers of fiction and makers of films may find themselves fascinated by such figures and even see in them the stuff of heroes. Historians are more cautious. Perhaps, being bourgeois types, they fear that their colleagues will consider them frivolous or perverse.

Pierre-François Lacenaire, poet and assassin, was convicted of a sordid double murder and a bungled attempt at a third. While in prison awaiting trial, he became an instant celebrity: he presided at press conferences crowded with journalists; he received a stream of eminent visitors, including writers who recorded his *bons mots* and phrenologists who measured the bumps on his head and made his life mask; he was swamped with messages and gifts from ladies of the best society (one of whom asked for his vital statistics—date of birth, age, date of first murder—to use as lucky numbers in the lottery). Lacenaire wrote poetry and read the classics. According to Victor Hugo, he made a disciple of his jailer, with whom he discussed serious literature and to whom he willed his personal library.

At his trial, Lacenaire dominated the proceedings. He confounded witnesses and refuted the testimony of his two accomplices who were desperately trying to deny complicity. He confessed all of his misdeeds in full detail, and at the end, electrified the courtroom with an hour-long improvised speech that outshone the arguments of all the lawyers. So self-possessed and good-tempered did he seem that rumors went round of some sort of plea-bargaining arrangement. Allegedly he was to be pardoned after conviction and then made chief of a special branch of the police. The example of Vidocq was fresh in men's minds. Indeed, Lacenaire boasted that he had found much of his inspiration in Vidocq's memoirs.

After his conviction, Lacenaire in turn wrote his memoirs. With some of his poems, they were published soon after his execution and became a best-seller. Potboiler biographies of Lacenaire kept appearing over the next thirty years. Stendhal planned to include him in a novel (which, however, was never finished). Dostoevsky read of the case and became so intrigued that he copied Lacenaire's crime almost to the last detail in *Crime and Punishment*. In the 1860s the leading French encyclopedia devoted five solid columns to Lacenaire's career—almost as much as it gave to Lafayette. If we are to believe the poet Gautier, the writer Maxime du Camp somehow obtained Lacenaire's severed right hand after the execution, had it embalmed, and displayed the grisly relic on a cushion in his drawing room.

Then, for several decades, Lacenaire went into eclipse, his crimes and his name forgotten. It was André Breton, chief doctrinaire of the surrealist school, who rediscovered him in the 1920s and acclaimed him one of the surrealists' heroes. They found in Lacenaire a strain of bizarre black humor, along with a total rejection of the complacent bourgeois world. A new crop of popular books followed. Marcel Carné reincarnated him as one of the major characters in his classic film of 1945, *Les Enfants du Paradis*. A Parisian editor in 1968 brought out a new edition of Lacenaire's memoirs, proclaiming him "a man of our own times." The BBC in London soon followed suit, dramatizing his life under the title "The Literate Killer."

How did this obscure figure manage to captivate so many people of his own and later generations and attain a kind of heroic stature? If Lacenaire was really "the first consciously professional criminal" (which is more than doubtful), his crimes hardly belong in the category of murder as one of the

Lacenaire in *Les Enfants du Paradis*.

fine arts. In fact, he and an accomplice were convicted for a brutal and amateurish butchery of a slum-dwelling transvestite and the latter's aged mother. Lacenaire thought, quite mistakenly, that the victims possessed a hoard of money. His second venture two weeks later was even less professional: with another accomplice, he lured a bank messenger to a false rendezvous and sought to rob him and slit his throat. This time the job was completely bungled, and the two malefactors had to flee empty-handed.

It was not his criminal style and genius, then, that won Lacenaire admiration; it was his personality as revealed during his nine-month imprisonment and his trial. His uninterrupted show of bravado, his obvious intelligence, his absolute cynicism combined to make him seem a unique phenomenon, and to some, a tragic hero. Literate, articulate, gracious, he was seen as the totally alienated intellectual who had declared his own personal war to the death on society—a society whose corruption, hypocrisy, and indifference to misery and oppression justified any ruthless acts that might undermine its rotten foundations.

From childhood, Lacenaire explained to his captivated listeners and readers, he had become convinced that human beings are fundamentally flawed, and that human nature has never changed. Support for this assessment he found (or thought he found) in his favorite reading—history. "Men are the same in every epoch; by observing what one man has done in given circumstances, you can anticipate what another man will do in like conditions." From his early teens, when he happened onto a guillotine erected in a public square in Lyon, he convinced himself that "an invisible bond existed between me and this frightful machine. . . . I became so habituated to this idea that I couldn't imagine dying in any other fashion."

Yet there runs through Lacenaire's memoirs another theme quite different from his professed alienation from humankind and from a rotten social edifice. That theme is familiar enough to students of modern psychiatry, but seems more startling in his time; it suggests that beneath this alienation, this cynical contempt for the world, there lay the most sensitive, the most generous, the most kindly nature one can imagine. Alas, these native tendencies were, if we are to believe Lacenaire's self-analysis, frustrated from earliest childhood by a narrow-minded, autocratic father and by an adored mother who openly preferred his older brother. Deprived thus of the parental affection for which he thirsted, harshly punished for a few peccadilloes, his misery was compounded by his experience at school. A series of brutal and obtuse teachers, jealous of his brilliant mind and his lack of deference, got him expelled from one school after another until his angry father cut off his education and condemned him to a humdrum clerical job.

All this, one might think, might have inspired Lacenaire's defense lawyer to call in the psychiatrists at his trial. Prima facie, it appears to be a textbook case of the effects of early frustration on a sensitive nature. But instead of psychiatrists, Lacenaire was to get phrenologists. Besides, some skeptics might suspect Lacenaire's self-analysis as the work of a twisted egoist, rationalizing his misdeeds by blaming home and school.

Adolescence and young manhood were to bring new misfortunes. Lacenaire drifted from one clerical job to another, chronically short of funds to support his self-confessed urge to join the big spenders. One employer accused him (unjustly, he claimed) of stealing from the till. Somewhat later, gambling debts forced him to leave town in a hurry. He joined the army for a time, then deserted. Arriving in Paris, he sought to make a new start in life but, in his own words, "was refused a place at the banquet." Jobless, hungry, and frustrated, his self-pity overwhelmed any vestiges of his better nature. Heretofore, he recalled, he had been contemptuous of his fellow men but had not detested them. Now hatred consumed him. "To kill without remorse," he decided, "would be the greatest of pleasures." But the joy of killing for its own sake was not enough; his real purpose was to become "the scourge of society." "It was the very foundation of the social edifice that I wanted to attack." He set out, therefore, to learn the trade of professional criminal. Reading Vidocq showed him that the real school of crime was the nineteenth-century prison. Accordingly, he got himself arrested for a minor offense and spent a year learning from the experts.

Lacenaire and his victim.

One wonders how much he really learned. Certainly the two jobs he tried to pull off in December 1834 were clumsy failures in both plan and execution. Murdering a couple of slum dwellers was not likely to shake the social edifice. He expected a rich haul, of course, but he had followed a false lead. If his exploit had succeeded, he later insisted, he would not have become a *bon bourgeois* enjoying his wealth, but would have followed the model of Robin Hood, succoring the poor and redoubling his efforts to destroy a rotten society. Whether or not this was genuine, it won him admiring applause as he held court in prison while awaiting trial.

"If I have one quality that's absolutely beyond dispute, it is courage. I have never known fear." Was it courage or bravado that carried him triumphantly through his imprisonment, his trial, and even his rendezvous with the guillotine? No one can say for certain. The execution, in any case, was an event. "There is much talk in the Paris salons," declared the august *Revue des Deux Mondes*, "of certain women who prolonged the pleasures of the ball until dawn in order to attend the execution." Although the place and time had been kept strictly confidential, the *Revue* complained that these ladies had used their high connections to break the secret. At the foot of the guillotine, Lacenaire provided the crowd with a good show. He waved in friendly fashion to the chief of police, thanked him without irony for coming out, and asked whether the detective who had arrested him would be in attendance. His nerve held up, it would appear, until the blade fell. Some newspaper reports alleged that his bravado had cracked at the end and that he had died as a cringing coward. But Lacenaire's admirers insisted that these stories were planted by the government, which feared that a true account would reinforce his status as popular hero and would inspire others to a life of crime. Whatever one's attitude toward Lacenaire, there is reason to believe that he played out his role to the end.

Pierre Rivière was a quite different type: a barely literate farm boy who had never left the immediate vicinity of his native Norman village and who was regarded there as a kind of harmless madman, almost in the class of village idiot. Some of his behavior since childhood had been sufficiently odd to encourage this belief: he nailed frogs to a wall, pretending that he was reenacting the crucifixion; he raced through the fields, fighting sham battles (in which he sliced off the heads of cabbages); he liked to scare younger children. The brief memoir that he wrote in prison after his arrest lacked the literary polish of Lacenaire's, yet it remains a rather remarkable document to come from the pen of a young and probably subnormal peasant. It began with brusque directness: "I, Pierre Rivière, having slaughtered my mother, my sister, and my brother . . ." Most of what we know about this obscure figure comes from this curious memoir and from testimony at his trial.

His was another case of an unhappy childhood, an abnormal family relationship that led to a calculated crime. Unlike Lacenaire, young Rivière hated rather than loved his mother— not so much because she lacked affection for him, but because she was a real village virago who made his father's life almost unbearable. Rivière senior seems to have been a placid and inoffensive type who was hounded and henpecked without mercy by his wife. Young Pierre brooded over his father's miserable fate and decided at last that it was his duty as a son to save him. Like Lacenaire, he drew inspiration from history. He had read a few simple texts about ancient Rome and France's past and had been deeply impressed by a series of heroic figures who had won glory and immortality by dying for a great cause. These self-sacrificing idealists would be his models. Destiny dictated that he exterminate the source of trouble by doing away with his mother and, for good measure, his sister, who was the maternal favorite. More strangely, however, he added his younger brother to the hit list, even though that child was his father's favorite. Pierre's reasoning was ingenious if twisted: his purpose, he declared, was to reduce his father's burden of suffering. If he, Pierre, were to kill only his mother and sister, thus obviously sacrificing his own life for his father's well-being, the father would grieve forever after over Pierre's execution. But if he slaughtered the paternal favorite as well, the father would rejoice rather than grieve when Pierre's head fell to the guillotine and could live out his last years with no pangs of regret. So it was that Pierre justified his action as he went about his bloody business, swinging a pruning hook with deadly effectiveness.

His purpose accomplished, Rivière made no real attempt to get away. He went off into the neighboring woods, slept in the open (as was often his habit), and wandered about the area for a full month before someone recognized and reported him. He made no effort to deny what he had done; rather, he asked for quick justice and the death penalty. His detention and trial, in contrast to Lacenaire's, attracted little publicity and no crowds of admirers or sensation seekers. But psychiatrists *were* called to testify in his case, and, as might be expected, they gave contradictory opinions about his sanity. The jury's verdict was death by the guillotine, as Rivière had wished. But there was enough evidence of bizarre behavior to lead some influential citizens and local officials to appeal to King Louis-Philippe for mercy, and Rivière's sentence was commuted at the last moment to life imprisonment. He served five years before committing suicide in his cell.

The whole affair drew little public notice at the time. Outside the immediate region both the man and the incident were promptly forgotten. For over a century the record lay buried in the judicial archives and the moldering newspapers, until it was disinterred in the 1970s by Michel Foucault and his seminar students at the Collège de France. In 1973 they published a volume containing Rivière's memoir, the relevant court records, and some elaborate commentaries by both Foucault and his disciples. Foucault confessed to a fascination with this primitive figure out of the obscure past. In his own words, he "fell under the spell of the parricide with the reddish-brown eyes."

To the Foucault circle, Rivière was neither a brutal monster nor the pitiful victim of hallucinations, but a tragic hero whose deed carried a symbolic quality of world-historical dimension. By his desperate act, they insist, he expressed the outrage of all ordinary men against the "suffocation" of modern existence, against "the mute horror of the daily round, the rule of lies, the foul machine that crushes the disinherited of the earth." Rivière "killed and consented to die so that amid the deadly

Moi, Pierre Rivière,
ayant égorgé ma mère,
ma sœur et mon frère...
de
René Allio

Cahiers du Cinéma, November 1976.

immobility of existence something would happen, would begin to live, to move, to question, to disturb." His wielding of the pruning hook was a blow for freedom "against the timelessness of oppression and the order of power." In the Foucaultian view, Rivière's heroic act called for the pen of a Plutarch. None being available, the French cineast René Allio came forward as substitute. His filmed portrayal of the episode—laboring under the unwieldy title *I, Pierre Rivière, having Slaughtered my Mother, my Sister, and my Brother . . .*—was a faithful, even literal, transposition of the Rivière memoir onto film. The apotheosis, though long delayed, thus became complete.

Pierre-François Lacenaire and Pierre Rivière lived, killed, and died at the height of the romantic era in Europe. No doubt it was the mood of the times that bred so much eccentric talk about "the metaphysics of crime" and "murder as a fine art" and that aroused such avid public interest in the criminal underworld. The climate of romanticism in the early nineteenth century may also explain why an embittered quasi intellectual like Lacenaire was lionized, while a crude country bumpkin like Rivière, swinging a deadly pruning hook, went unnoticed. The latter's crime lacked finesse, and the criminal himself lacked flair. Glamorizing such a deed and such a man would seem difficult if not impossible.

But how is one to understand the rediscovery in our own day of such characters as these two assassins, and especially the elevation of the peasant Rivière to the pantheon of artistic killers and voices of social protest? Perhaps it proves nothing more than the morbid attraction exerted by murder and murderers, from Cain through Jack the Ripper to the most recent mass strangler. But it may suggest also a resurgence of the romantic mood in one of its more perverse forms: the mood that finds "bourgeois" conformity the most nauseous of traits, that not only understands but glorifies alienation of spirit, and that claims to discover in the most violent forms of protest— arson, murder, terrorism—evidence of true greatness of soul.

Portrait-caricature of Lamartine by Nadar.

3

A Poet in Politics: or,
How Revolutions
Devour Their Children

REVOLUTIONS, LIKE OCEAN STORMS, are likely to uproot strange specimens from the lower depths. It is rare, however, for a revolutionary tempest to sweep a poet into power—and least likely of all, a romantic poet. An aura of romanticism suffused the events of 1848 in Europe—the greatest revolutionary year of the nineteenth century—and it was most dramatically embodied in the figure of Alphonse de Lamartine. Few men have risen so high, and fallen so far and so fast. In February Lamartine emerged overnight, out of the wreckage of the French monarchy, to become both symbol and leader of the provisional republic. In April the nation swept him to an almost unprecedented triumph at the polls. In eleven electoral districts, his name attracted the votes of two million Frenchmen—ten times the number received by any other candidate to the Constituent Assembly. Yet in December, when the voters chose their president by direct election, he suffered a humiliating defeat, running a miserable last in a field of five candidates, and polling a mere two-tenths of one percent of the ballots cast.

To understand the events of 1848, one must begin by trying to understand the man. But here, at the very outset, the difficulties begin. No two biographers of Lamartine agree about him, and from none of them do we get a convincing, clearly focused portrait. Historians are notorious, of course, for their disagreements about men and events. But where Lamartine is involved the contradictions run rampant. These differences, moreover, were shared by his contemporaries. As we read what men of his time had to say about him, and even what Lamartine had to say about himself, his figure, instead of coming more clearly into focus, grows steadily more indistinct. Even Karl Marx, who found it easy to categorize the politicians of his time and the class interests they served, was baffled: "Lamartine," he wrote, "represented no real interest, no particular class; he was the February Revolution personified, with its illusions, its poetry, its fine phrases." One begins at last to suspect that the cloudiness of vision of the historians and biographers reflects a cloudiness in the man's own nature.

When Lamartine entered politics in 1833, at the age of forty-three, he was already immortal—at least as defined by the French. He was the youngest member of the Académie Française (popularly known as the Forty Immortals). Already, for a decade, he had been one of the lions of the literary salons, and he ranked among the glittering stars of French literature. No other French poet has ever won so large and passionate a following among what used to be called the fair sex. He and Lord Byron, said a contemporary, "turned the heads of at least a quarter of the feminine generation of their time." One married lady from the provinces who had the incredible luck of seeing Lamartine during a visit to Paris returned home in a state of ecstasy, surrounded herself with portraits of the poet and with every edition of his works, and for ten years wrote him daily love letters—none of which was ever mailed.

Yet poetry bored Lamartine, despite the acclaim that it

brought him and despite the almost inhuman ease with which he could dash off lyrics. Toward the end of his life, when his godson shyly confessed that he too was writing poetry, Lamartine exploded: "Verses! Do you mean to say you're scribbling verses, wretch? Can't you see where it has brought me? Never go in for literature. Become a farmer, a diplomat, anything at all; but at least do something serious." "Poetry for me," he remarked to a friend in the midst of the 1848 upheaval, "was never anything but a passing distraction. My spirit has always been devoted to the great, the serious matters of politics." His nagging fear was that people would not take a poet seriously—and in this he was not entirely wrong. Most of his contemporaries continued to identify him with the drawing that appeared in his first great poetic success, *Jocelyn:* it portrayed a Byronesque youth with flowing hair and eyes turned to heaven, plucking a harp as he sat beside a fog-enshrouded lake. Yet he could never force himself to abandon poetry, if only because he was always in desperate need of funds to live in the style of an aristocrat in Paris.

When Lamartine first was elected to parliament in 1833, his voters assumed that they were choosing a solid monarchist of the most traditional sort. The Lamartines had been loyal supporters of the now-exiled Bourbon dynasty; young Lamartine himself had resigned his diplomatic post in 1830 rather than serve "the usurper," Louis-Philippe. Yet when a friend asked him whether he intended to sit on the right or the left in the Chamber of Deputies, he answered enigmatically, "On the ceiling." The hall was crowded when he made his first appearance, and he gave the audience a fine dramatic performance. He entered on the arm of the old Marquis de Lafayette, the very symbol of republicanism, and the republicans cheered him to the echo. But as Lafayette turned to take his seat on the left benches, Lamartine kept on walking—past the left, past the center, past even the Bourbon supporters, taking his seat at last in splendid isolation at the farthest right end of the front bench. All observers agreed that there was a world of symbolism here—if only they could decide what was symbolized.

Just where he stood politically remained unclear during the

fifteen years that followed, and Lamartine did his best to perpetuate the mystery. His program, he declared, was simple enough for anyone to grasp: conservatism and progress. He was, he declared, "an aristocrat holding out his hand to a powerless democracy that has fallen into a ditch." At one point he announced the foundation of a movement called "the Social party"; but a colleague was not far wrong in remarking, as Lamartine entered the Chamber alone, "Here comes the Social party." He continued to sit all alone on the far right, but refused to take a stand either for or against the existing monarchy.

Frenchmen found it hard to understand this paradoxical character, but many of them were fascinated. Indeed, Lamartine himself seems to have shared that fascination. He quickly built a reputation as the most remarkable orator in parliament. His style, modeled on that of the Roman spellbinder Cicero, specialized in grandiloquence, amplification, and prolixity. He flooded the Chamber with his purple and gold rhetoric. "I wager," he remarked to a friend, "that I could speak for two or three hours on any subject you may want to mention." He could, and did. No issue fazed him. "Did you ever take the trouble to study economics?" he asked his friend Sainte-Beuve. "About a week ago I stuck my nose into it for the first time, and it's as easy as saying *bonjour;* it takes no effort at all." Shortly afterwards, he spoke magnificently on the interest rate on government bonds—though friends noticed that he was still totally incapable of adding a column of figures. The flood of eloquence hypnotized many of his listeners. When he was scheduled to speak, the public galleries were jammed with the social elite. The more hardened politicians were, however, more difficult to please; they complained that his speeches were empty, his ideas confused, and his style nauseating. The king's chief minister, Guizot, the most unpoetic of politicians, finally exploded: *"C'est une machine détraquée!"* (roughly, "He's off his rocker").

Baffling and contradictory though he was, Lamartine by the mid-1840s enjoyed a kind of prestige that was quite unique. His isolation added to his glamour; he seemed to stand above the squalor of party squabbles. His aloofness was reinforced

Portrait de Lamartine by Louis-François Decainse.

by a gradual withdrawal from active political life. After 1843 he rarely appeared in the Chamber, and he spoke more rarely still. Somehow—perhaps through the poet's intuition—he foresaw the crisis of the regime and his own impending destiny. "I can see where France is heading," he wrote to a friend; "I shall be there waiting, ten years ahead of her." In February 1843 he wrote to his niece: "Both the right and the left keep appealing to me to become their leader. They are going to make me a great force in the country five years hence." It was five years later almost to the day that Lamartine was to be called to lead a nascent republic.

Perhaps the most startling thing about this curious genius, as one rereads what he said and wrote during that prerevolutionary decade, was the way in which he managed to combine intuitive understanding and fatuous, almost childlike vanity. On the one hand, he could divine the collapse of a seemingly stable monarchy and could position himself to be called in as a national savior. He could even detect, beneath the prosperous crust of bourgeois France, evidence of serious social tensions. He could speak, unlike most members of the governing elite, about such things as misery and injustice, about the dangers of excessive wealth and power concentrated into too few hands, about the "horrible volcano" of proletarian discontent. It was only his own self-image that was sometimes ludicrously distorted. Thus this man whose personal finances were always chaotic could solemnly address himself to a young visitor: "Young man, look carefully at this forehead of mine, and realize that you have seen the world's greatest financial brain." And to one of his acquaintances: "Perhaps I have lacked genius (I say this even though I doubt it), but sound judgment—never!"

While he waited beside the road for France to catch up with him, Lamartine lived the life of a Parisian celebrity. His house on the rue de l'Université was a buzzing center of the intellectual world. An enormous correspondence poured in daily from all over Europe. Each morning at four o'clock, long before the city was awake, he rose to toil until daylight at the verses that flowed so easily from his pen and kept him from utter financial disaster. Lavish and generous to a fault, he always spent the advance royalties from his next volume before he had even begun to write it.

In the mid-1840s, Lamartine turned for the first time to a new literary medium—history. He proposed to his publisher an eight-volume study of the Great Revolution, focused on the moderate faction called the Girondins and designed to show that moderates could accomplish revolutionary change. The contract was signed for a quarter-million francs; it allowed him two years for the entire task, research as well as writing. The poet drove himself unsparingly toward his 1847 deadline. Once a friend noted during a conversation that Lamartine kept scribbling on a pad in his lap, and expressed curiosity. "Oh," remarked Lamartine negligently, "it's a chapter from *Les Girondins*." Boredom set in; a thousand times he would have burned the whole manuscript, had he not already spent the royalties. At last the deadline came and, miraculously, was met; and the day of publication made it all seem worthwhile. "The publishers tell me," he wrote triumphantly, "that there has never been such a success. . . . The most elegant ladies waited up all night to get their copies."

Lamartine's critics, then and later, protested that the work was not history but political poetry, or an eight-volume political speech. Rival historians charged that he had never set foot in the archives, but had consulted only his own imagination. The critic Sainte-Beuve said caustically that it should have been entitled *Les Lamartines* rather than *Les Girondins*, since every heroic figure in it was the author under a different name. Yet survivors of the Revolutionary era agreed that Lamartine had somehow caught and expressed the spirit of the time. Even the historian Michelet, whose own book was eclipsed by Lamartine's, said ruefully that the poet seemed to have "the gift of divination without need for research." In Alexandre Dumas's admiring opinion, Lamartine had "raised history to the level of the novel."

The poet reveled in the praise, and ignored his critics. "What do I care for them!" he exclaimed; "the ladies and the young people are on my side; I can get along without the rest." He did, however, indignantly reject Chateaubriand's charge that he had glorified violence by "gilding the guillotine." Yet *Les*

Girondins did contribute to the mounting crisis in France, and Lamartine did not regret it. "Everywhere," he wrote to a friend, "it is said that I have lighted the fire of great revolutions and have aroused the people for revolutions to come. May God so will it!" The revolution he sought would, however, be a moderate and sensible one; in later years he was to argue that his book alone had prevented 1848 from degenerating into another reign of terror.

The success of *Les Girondins* inspired great enthusiasm in Mâcon, Lamartine's hometown in Burgundy. Its citizens proposed to erect a statue of their favorite son; Lamartine refused, but agreed to accept instead a public banquet in his honor. On a hot July day in 1847, three thousand diners assembled at outdoor tables, under a two-acre canvas canopy. As the guest of honor rose to speak, a violent thunderstorm struck. Gusts of wind tore the canvas to ribbons. The diners sat in a drenching cloudburst, but no one left his place. Lamartine rose above the elements—lightning flashing about his head, torn bits of his phrases floating out to the audience between thunderbolts. If no one afterwards could reconstruct the whole speech, at least one phrase did stick: "It will fall, this royalty, be sure of that. . . . We have had the revolution of freedom and the counterrevolution of glory; now we shall have the revolution of contempt." Some years earlier, Lamartine had coined another phrase: "France is bored." Now he seemed to be issuing a call to action against the dullness of a prosaic age. Since public political meetings were illegal, moderate reformers and republicans evaded the rules by organizing banquets at which political speeches followed the main course. A rash of such affairs spread across the land, and invitations poured in upon Lamartine to appear as the featured speaker. But he withdrew once more into his self-chosen solitude, sending his regrets to the organizers of the banquets, reserving himself for his imminent rendezvous with destiny.

His moment arrived at last in February 1848. On the eleventh, he broke an eighteen-month silence in the Chamber, rising to flay the regime for its mistakes. The government, irritated by the wave of criticism, struck back by forbidding a political banquet scheduled to be held in Paris itself. Although Lamartine was not one of the organizers, he threw his support to those who wished to ignore the government's ban. When they wavered, he cried dramatically: "Whatever the rest of you may do, I shall go to the banquet, even if only my shadow is there to follow me!" But he was spared the trouble; in place of the forbidden banquet, the government got a spontaneous revolution. Street demonstrations began on the twenty-second. Workers, students, shopkeepers joined in, encouraged by the opposition press. The crowd called for reform, and the dismissal of the king's chief minister, Guizot. The king complied on the twenty-third, but it was too late. A bloody clash between demonstrators and an army unit infuriated the protesters. By the morning of the twenty-fourth Paris was in the hands of the rebels. As they smashed into the royal palace, Louis-Philippe and the queen departed hastily for English exile.

Parliament, confused and divided, met that afternoon in emergency session. A growing crowd outside was pressing at the entrances and calling for a republic. Although the king had abandoned power, the royal family had not yet given up: the heir apparent, Louis-Philippe's nine-year-old grandson, had arrived at the Chamber with his mother, the Duchesse d'Orléans, who hoped to be named regent for her son. As they waited in the wings, Lamartine rose to speak. In a magnificent flight of elocution, he extolled the courage of that royal pair—the touching spectacle of a duchess defending her rights and those of her innocent son (cheers and tears from the monarchist deputies on the right). But then his tone changed imperceptibly. The moment was critical, he said; the time had come for a new era; a regency could no longer unite the nation; a provisional government must be formed instead (ovation from the left). At the same moment the crowd smashed its way into the building with cries of "Long live the republic! To the Hôtel de Ville! Let Lamartine lead us!" And off they went, in accordance with old tradition, to that symbolic capitol of French republicanism.

The monarchy had fallen, but no one could yet be sure that

Lamartine addressing the crowd at the Hôtel de Ville in 1848. *Illustrated London News,* April 22, 1848.

the republic had taken its place. The crowd of some sixty thousand outside the Hôtel de Ville wanted to be certain; its leaders recalled that in 1830 their revolution had been confiscated by the Orleanists. Seven times during that afternoon and evening, the crowd sent delegations into the building to demand assurances from the provisional government; seven times Lamartine took on the task of pacifying the people. From the balcony he spoke to them, calm and eloquent in all the confusion, lecturing them on the meaning of liberty. Each time they cheered his words, went away mollified, then began to wonder what he had really said, and sent a new delegation to find out. At last, toward midnight, they got their way: the provisional government proclaimed the republic to the delirious crowd. Lamartine, exhausted but jubilant, set out on foot for home, followed by a cheering crowd of workers and students. Long after he had retired for the night, the patriots continued to demonstrate outside his door, until at last he had to rise and harangue them again from the window. A timeworn plaque on the front of his house still informs the curious passerby that "Here, on the night of February 24, 1848, Lamartine spoke to the people of Paris."

Until that date, Lamartine had never claimed to be a republican. If he was a late and somewhat reluctant convert, he now accepted his new identity with enthusiasm. He dashed off a letter to a friend in the provinces, announcing the news in a fine burst of Lamartinian prose: "The republic is founded, new, pure, holy, immortal, popular and transcendent, peaceful and great!" His motives in adopting the republic—his conversion in the heat of revolution—have been variously interpreted. He himself later explained that the monarchy had lost its appeal, that the only remaining barrier to anarchy was the republic. His critics believed that he deliberately blocked the proclamation of a regency because of his thirst for popularity and power, which could never be fully gratified if he were forced to stand in the shadow of a regent or a king. Whatever moved him, his decision did make him the key figure in the new republic.

Technically, he was merely one among equals in the provisional government, holding the single portfolio of foreign affairs. But in fact, he was spokesman, symbol, and leader all in one. His popularity during those early weeks was immense. A few days after the revolution, a crowd of forty thousand followed him down the boulevard crying (somewhat to his embarrassment), "Long live First Consul Lamartine!" Souvenir hunters ripped at his clothing as he passed; he lost three coats in short order. As always, the most intense adulation came from female admirers, who swarmed about this handsome, slightly ethereal tribune of the people, to be saluted with the chaste republican kiss on the forehead that was the great man's greeting to the leaders of feminine delegations. The acclaim was dizzying, and raised him to a state of prodigious exaltation. "I see myself as a real miracle," he wrote to a friend. "I can't go out in public without inspiring a riot of love."

So delirious a love affair between poet and people could hardly last for long. Emotional jags are fatiguing, and glamour fades with time. Besides, rival factions quickly emerged in the new republic and polarized around two competing ideologies. On one side stood the moderates and libertarians, dedicated to political reform; on the other, the radicals, socialists, and egalitarians—committed to social reform and experimentation as well. Should the new republic adopt the bourgeois principle of laissez-faire, freeing the individual citizen to make his own way to wealth and success? Or should it seek to create a new kind of society, a welfare state ahead of its time, protecting the weak, guaranteeing employment to all those willing to work, transforming the system into one based on cooperation and workers' control of production?

Some cautious moves toward social reform were made during the early weeks, and there was a great deal of talk about more sweeping change. Ordinary citizens were filled with zeal as they sought to reshape human destiny. The French archives contain a massive file of more than seven thousand petitions and proposals to the government of 1848—for such things as abolition of the death penalty, reform of the prisons, even what we today would call zero population growth, as well as a scheme to "abolish begging, prostitution, and the proletariat" and a modest blueprint for "a new system of civilization."

For a time, the rival forces coexisted within the government. But eventually, in June, their antagonism was to produce a bloody civil war. Perhaps the intensity of these popular hopes and dreams ruled out any workable compromise between the ideological factions and made a violent climax inevitable. Yet it is at least possible that strong and able leadership might have managed to find a way out. For the student of Lamartine, here is the central issue: was he in a position to avert a violent crisis? How hard did he try, and how near did he come to success? Was his failure the product of his own mistakes and shortcomings, or of events beyond any leader's control?

On Lamartine's role in 1848, historians as well as contemporaries have ranged from one extreme to the other. To one group of critics, Lamartine was almost ludicrously devoid of the qualities of crisis leadership. How, they ask, could a fog-bound poet, vain and muddleheaded and drunk on his own popularity, offer the nation any kind of guidance at all? Such a man, they contend, could do no more than stumble along from one political pothole to the next, sublimely unaware of his own confusion, until at last the nation awakened to his incapacity and turned him out in something worse than a revolution of contempt—a revolution of ridicule.

A second hostile group has portrayed him as cunning instead of confused, hypocritical rather than fatuous. His real significance, they argue, lay in his role as spokesman or lightning rod for the possessing classes, as defender of the sacred rights of property and special privilege against the proponents of social justice. By his purple oratory and his democratic double-talk, they allege, Lamartine could easily mislead the masses and manipulate the state machinery until he and his cohorts felt strong enough to break the back of social reform. Then, when he was no longer useful, the "party of order" cynically jettisoned him in favor of more ruthless leaders.

Still a third category of contemporaries and later scholars, considerably fewer in number, find Lamartine neither ridiculous nor contemptible. At bottom, they contend, he was a sincere and high-minded intellectual—perhaps impractical and vain, as so many intellectuals are, yet a man whose grasp of public affairs and whose understanding of human aspirations were no less genuine for being intuitive. True, he belonged to the possessing classes, and shared with them their fear of violence and confiscation. But, unlike them, he could also understand the viewpoints of the reformer and the proletarian; he perceived the depth of their discontent, and knew that only concessions by the rich and powerful could avert disaster. By trying to straddle, by seeking to preserve the initial alliance between moderates and social reformers, he consciously risked the fury of the more bigoted conservatives, who cried betrayal. If the argument is sound, it might follow that moderates in our own day ought to recognize in Lamartine a spiritual ancestor and a misunderstood statesman, one of that long line of middle-of-the-roaders whose common fate it is to be misunderstood, and finally to be crushed between two extremes.

Each of these three interpretations can be defended with at least some plausibility. Lamartine fits no pigeonhole exactly, and to wrestle with the conflicting evidence is a fascinating exercise in historical judgment. But the most intriguing of the three theories is the view of Lamartine as tragic hero—in part because it is the case least often argued by historians, and the least doctrinaire in spirit. The more orthodox explanations— Lamartine as vacuous intellectual or as two-faced bigot—may be left to the standard works.

Lamartine became aware in March 1848 that his honeymoon with the people was coming to an end. Left-wing activists, although they had some representation in the provisional government, were growing obstreperous—organizing, demonstrating, demanding more power and speedier action. Alongside the cry "Vive Lamartine!" there were now as many cries for radical leaders like the democratic tribune Ledru-Rollin or the utopian socialist Louis Blanc. The activists pressed not only for immediate social reforms but also for an aggressively ideological foreign policy. Revolution was spreading now throughout much of the continent, and the radicals demanded a French crusade on behalf of the resurgent Hungarians and Poles and Italians.

Lamartine neither challenged the radicals head-on nor capitulated to their pressure. His choice was to temporize, to use persuasion and diplomacy, in an effort to preserve the governing coalition of moderates and radicals. He kept Ledru-Rollin in the government and sought to win his cooperation in a policy of gradualism; he arranged dramatic secret meetings with such fire-eaters as the professional revolutionary Blanqui, in an effort to talk them out of a resort to violence. As foreign minister, he issued grandiloquent foreign-policy statements that began like Don Quixote and ended like Sancho Panza. But at the same time, he was aware that appeasement of the left might not succeed and that the radical wing might yet resort to force. Therefore he quietly arranged for the creation of a new armed police, the *garde mobile*, made up of well-paid recruits from the working class. (Karl Marx charged that it was recruited from the dregs of the Parisian *lumpenproletariat*, urban riffraff that would take on any dirty job if paid enough. A recent analysis shows, however, that the *garde mobile* was drawn from the same varied base as the regular police.)

When the first test of strength came in mid-April, and the radicals staged a monster street demonstration that might easily have turned into a new revolution, Lamartine's strategy proved itself effective. Ledru-Rollin stood with the government in defense of public order, and Blanqui, the street fighter par excellence, failed to appear in the streets at all. Meanwhile, the new *garde mobile* patrolled the streets in silent warning against any resort to force. That night, when it was all over, Lamartine's usually sardonic friend Sainte-Beuve told him emotionally, "Today, you were greater than Napoleon." Lamartine readily agreed.

During this tense period, Lamartine's cautious foreign policy assured the republic of a breathing spell to work out its crucial problems. His refusal to embark on a continental crusade for freedom, in the view of some later critics, showed him to be a forebear of Neville Chamberlain. The British historian A.J.P. Taylor, for example, has described Lamartine's foreign policy as the first step on a long road of abdication that led eventually to Munich; and a French scholar has added that if Lamartine had sent the French armies marching out in all directions for the cause of liberty, France would have been spared most of her later disasters—the June Days of 1848, plus 1870, 1914, and 1940. It is likely, however, that a French crusade in 1848 would have been a quixotic venture—that it would have crystallized a hostile European coalition, which might have strangled the new republic in infancy.

Late in April, on Easter Sunday, the nation had its first chance to speak when it went to the polls to elect a Constituent Assembly. The radicals had urged postponement of the elections until they might have time to "educate" the inexperienced peasant masses; but the moderate ministers, some of them through idealism and others through calculation, had refused any delay. Whatever the real motives, the outcome was an overwhelming victory for the moderates over the radicals and a staggering personal triumph for Lamartine (moderate republicans numbered about five hundred in the new Assembly, monarchists three hundred, and radicals only eighty). This marked the peak of Lamartine's career: two million Frenchmen, in eleven districts, cast their ballots in his name.

Yet only a month later, Lamartine was sliding rapidly toward political extinction. The new Assembly, dominated by moderates and conservatives, came roaring in determined to clear the defeated radicals out of all positions of power and to repeal the considerable body of social reforms (such as a guarantee of the right to a job, encouragement of cooperatives, abolition of debtors' prisons) that had been adopted to appease them. All that Lamartine needed to do to ensure his preeminence in the republic—even to become a kind of legal dictator, if he so desired—was to go along with this majority of his own political kin. But to the Assembly's amazement and fury, he demurred.

To push the radical representatives out of the government, Lamartine insisted, would be both dangerous and wrong; he demanded that the coalition be preserved. In the end he even announced bluntly that unless that symbol of radicalism Ledru-Rollin were included in the new five-man executive commission, he himself would refuse to serve. This was a kind of blackmail, and the Assembly resented it. Ledru and Lamartine were grudgingly elected to the executive commission, but they ranked only fourth and fifth in the order of voting. The moderates concluded that Lamartine was either dizzy with success or was playing a demagogic game to win radical support for his ambition to be president of the republic.

Worse was yet to come. When the Assembly repealed the social reform measures adopted since February, Lamartine argued and voted against the action. Indeed, he not only opposed the abolition of the National Workshops, which provided temporary jobs for the unemployed, but contended that these workers should be given long-term security by nationalizing the railways and shifting workshop employees to railroad jobs on the state payroll. More shocking still, he put forward the idea of a graduated income tax. Lamartine's support among the property owners quickly evaporated; he could only hope that the left still trusted him enough to hear his appeals against violence. But that proved a vain hope. When the Assembly in June carried out its threat to abolish the National Workshops and ordered recipients of the dole either to join the army or to work at the dangerous job of swamp-draining in the provinces, the workers and their allies turned to armed resistance as their only recourse. At least some conservative politicians welcomed this development; it seemed to provide an excuse for breaking the power of the "reds" in Paris and reassuring the defenders of social order.

When the barricades began to go up on June 23, Lamartine made a final desperate effort to head off a bloody showdown. He toured the city and pleaded with the embattled rebels, but without success. Failing in this, he urged General Cavaignac, the army commander in Paris, to clear the streets at once before a full-scale civil war could break out. The general, whose contempt for poets and other intellectuals was vast, ignored him. Instead, he gave the rebels a couple of days to dig in firmly, so that he might move up artillery and methodically blast them out of their strongholds. Such tactics had worked in Algeria; they worked again here, with savage results. At least fifteen hundred rebels were killed on the barricades or in the settling of accounts that followed, and unofficial estimates put the figure at three thousand or more. Lamartine later suspected, however, that Cavaignac had ulterior motives—that he purposely gave the rebellion time to grow to dangerous proportions so that the Assembly in panic would suspend the powers of the civilian executive and call in a military savior. This, at any rate, is exactly what the Assembly did.

RUE St ANTOINE

Rue St. Antoine, during the June Days, 1848. *Charivari*, August 18, 1848.

This three-day civil war in Paris, known as the June Days, was one of the bloodiest episodes in the history of modern France; it abruptly ended Lamartine's political career. His prestige collapsed; thereafter he was ignored, or treated with contempt, or even slandered in the crudest fashion. Thus the rumor spread that he had used his office to plunder the public treasury of two million francs, whereas in fact he was a hundred thousand francs poorer for his months in power. Perhaps he still clung to the illusion that the people would be faithful to him and, if given the chance, would sweep him into the presidency. His critics see this illusion as the motive for his last great performance in the Assembly in October, when once again his oratorical flamboyance carried the house away in a kind of emotional orgy. In opposition to those who feared the common voters and who wanted parliament to choose the president, he made his dramatic appeal for popular election: "Let God and the people speak!" But the common portrait of the fatuous poet, dreaming of vindication at the polls, is only partially convincing. Lamartine refused to enter his name formally as a candidate, although he hoped that the appeal of his name might still bring a symbolic vote of a half million or so from a grateful nation. He even voted against himself—and for General Cavaignac.

Neither Lamartine nor many other Frenchmen foresaw just how ungrateful the nation could be, or how much influence a dark horse with a famous name might have on the outcome. Among the candidates was Louis-Napoleon Bonaparte, nephew of the great Napoleon. Most of his life had been spent in political exile, interrupted only by two comic-opera attempts to invade France along with a few followers in an effort to restore the empire. Midway through 1848 he had again returned from England—legally this time—and had won a seat in the Assembly at a by-election. Most observers considered him a mere adventurer and even a buffoon, but they failed to judge the powerful attraction of his name, embellished by the growth since 1815 of the Napoleonic legend. God may have remained neutral in the presidential campaign, but the people's voice was clear: 5,500,000 votes were cast for Louis-Napoleon; 1,500,000 for Cavaignac; 500,000 for Ledru-Rollin; 37,000 for

LE JUGEMENT DE PARIS.
(Caricature imitée du **Punch**, le Charivari **de Londres**)

The candidates for the 1848 election (Lamartine, second from right). *Charivari,* November 18, 1848.

another radical, Raspail; and a paltry 17,910 for Lamartine. When the results were read out in the Assembly, a burst of derisive laughter greeted the Lamartine debacle. The poet, aware of the Assembly's vindictive mood, had chosen not to attend the session.

Victor Hugo, who went to call on Lamartine about this time, was shocked at his appearance. He had aged ten years in as many months, Hugo thought; his hair had turned white. Yet Hugo found him "generous and resigned." Six months later came a further blow; Lamartine's own home district of Mâcon rejected him as its deputy in the new legislature. Although another district later chose him in a by-election, it was small consolation. He was through in politics, and he knew it. He turned back once more (as political has-beens often do) to the writing of history—including his own. Although he sought to justify himself and to explain away his mistakes, he managed to persuade few readers. "No hero," wrote the British ambassador in Paris, "ever lost so much by choosing to be his own historian." Somehow he could never see himself clearly, even in retrospect. What he wrote only put further weapons into the hands of his enemies.

Nothing is easier than to lampoon a man like Lamartine. Perhaps that is why it has been so often done. It is harder to defend and justify this strange poet-statesman, caught up and tossed about by the storms of revolution. Perhaps, therefore, it is best to let him speak in his own behalf. Four years after his humiliation, he could still look back without rancor and could write with pride though also with a heavy dose of poetic license: "The times called for a resolute and devoted man to check a people bent on self-destruction. I took that task upon myself, and, whatever anyone may say, I did not think for a moment of myself, but only of the nation. I preserved France from war, crimes, blood, spoliation, anarchy. I put representative government back on its feet. . . . Since then, I have accepted obscurity, calumny, threats, prison, the scaffold[!] . . . What more can you ask? Ten times I could have made myself dictator, president, but it would have meant bloodshed, treason, homicide. At that price—never!"

Twenty-one years after the events of 1848, a French encyclopedia tells us, Lamartine died—"in poverty, a bit forgotten." Time and posterity have not done much better by him. He remains a bit forgotten by his countrymen, and even by the historians. Paris contains a tiny square named for him, and a street that is barely two blocks long. Perhaps this is the likely fate of a romantic poet who strays into the jungle of revolutionary politics. Perhaps this is what people mean when they speak of poetic justice.

Clemenceau by Edouard Manet.

4

Two Statesmen in
an Age of Complacency: or,
Idealism in Action

POLITICAL REGIMES, in the experience of Frenchmen, are evanescent things. According to an ancient anecdote, a Parisian bookseller, asked by a customer for a copy of the French constitution, answered acidly: "We don't deal in periodical literature." During the past two hundred years only one regime has outlasted a normal citizen's lifetime, and that one exception—the Third Republic (1870–1940)—was intended by most of its founders to be strictly temporary, a holding pattern until the return of a legitimate king. The reasons for its exceptional durability are complex, but surely one factor was detected by the Republic's first president, Adolphe Thiers, when he declared: "The republic is the regime that divides us least."

Two rival dynasties—Bourbon and Orleanist—together with two variants of the Napoleonic empire—those headed by Napoleon I and Napoleon III—had left a heritage of irreconcilable factionalism. The republic of 1848 had produced its factional divisions too, but somehow they seemed less intense. Liberty, Equality, Fraternity could provide a widely acceptable ideal—provided that Liberty, the individual's privilege to manage his own affairs, was assured clear primacy. In a nation where small- and medium-sized property was widely shared and where modest but steady economic growth had begun to seem a law of nature, a regime that rarely interfered with the individual citizen's daily life and property rights had considerable appeal. Most citizens might view their political leaders' posturing and game-playing with a certain ironic contempt, but at least the politicians usually left the "Middle Frenchman" alone. In such a system, garden-variety politicians seemed to be enough; there was no real need for statesmen. And in such an era, it was easy for bourgeois Frenchmen to become complacent, to forget or ignore the discontents of their less affluent fellows, to lose sight of the fact that change is an integral aspect of human affairs, a kind of law of history. For an idealist in politics, it was hardly a congenial time. Yet idealists persist in turning up, even at the most unpropitious moments.

Georges Clemenceau was the son of a doctor whose roots were in the most traditionalist part of France—the Vendée, where even today monarchists can at times be elected to office. Such a region, where reactionaries dominate the scene, is likely to breed a small but fanatical sect of flaming radicals. Clemenceau *père* was one of these: intensely republican, anticlerical, and chauvinistic—that odd combination that Frenchmen call the Jacobin tradition.

The younger Clemenceau, born in 1841 midway through the reign of Louis-Philippe and in the age of Balzac, absorbed this Jacobin faith from his father. Liberty, Equality, Fraternity for him was not a mere slogan but a living and attainable ideal. The Church he saw as the principal enemy of all that was reasonable and just, for it nurtured blind superstition and the defense of privilege. Throughout his life, he would denounce pro-Church politicians, whom he described as "buried up to the neck in priests." When he died at age eighty-eight, friends found on his bedside table his last reading matter—a history of the popes. This was not a case of late conversion; he had simply been looking for added evidence of evil and corruption.

Young Georges went to Paris in 1860 to study medicine and earned his degree in 1865. But in his off hours he went in for some modest political activism, joining the young republicans in small street demonstrations and serving a two-month jail sentence for putting up posters critical of Napoleon III. As a graduation present his father staked him to a trip to the United States; he arrived soon after the Civil War ended and stayed for four years. His favorite American politician was Thaddeus Stevens, the fire-eating antislavery congressman who proposed to treat the defeated Southern states as conquered provinces, to be occupied and reconstructed by Northern fiat—the right recipe, Clemenceau thought, for making the Southerners shape up. A brief visit to Richmond, however, shook Clemenceau's convictions; he was charmed by Southern manners, Southern belles, and the Virginia way of life. But he tore himself away from this corrupting atmosphere to settle for a time in New York, and then signed on to teach in an exclusive Connecticut girls' school, where he professed French and horsemanship. He promptly fell in love with one of his students, and eventually married her over strong family opposition. The marriage ended in separation, however, after only seven years. Thereafter, he became increasingly a loner in his personal life, a man with few friends and even fewer close relationships. One wonders how different his character might have been if he had enjoyed the consolations of wife and family instead of returning each evening to his austere bachelor apartment. Perhaps it would have made no difference, yet who can be sure?

Clemenceau returned to Paris just in time to witness the fall of Napoleon III. He was in the streets with the republican demonstrators on September 4, 1870, when the news came of the French army's defeat and the emperor's capture at Sedan. By evening the empire had given way to a provisional republic, and Clemenceau was appointed the next day to be mayor of the Montmartre quarter. This sudden eminence was brief; six months later, in March 1871, the violent episode of the Paris Commune brought what seemed to be an end to his political career.

The Commune was in large part an angry emotional response of Parisians to the policies of the new republican leaders, who had signed an armistice with the Germans and had moved the capital to Versailles. Parisian leftists set up an independent municipal regime, and rejected the conservative republic's authority. Clemenceau refused to take sides either with the Commune or with Versailles; he tried to mediate and to avert a bloody confrontation. But things had gone too far for compromise. Clemenceau was denounced by both factions, and was forced to resign the seat in the new National Assembly to which he had recently been elected. His political career seemed to have reached an inglorious end.

Yet he soon managed, for the first of several times in his career, to climb back from the pit of despair. After the Commune had been crushed, he won election to the new Paris city council from a working-class district, and he quickly consolidated his foothold there. Citizens were invited to bring their civic problems to his office. Two days a week he changed hats and provided free medical treatment to the voters. After five years of this double service, the district sent him to parliament, where he was to spend the next forty-four years (though with one long interruption).

It was natural for him to sit on the far left with the group known as the Radicals, which clung to the Jacobin heritage of ferocious anticlericalism and fervent patriotism. The Radicals also professed a belief in drastic political and social reforms such as abolition of the conservative Senate, a progressive income tax, and laws to protect labor. But over the years that followed, it became increasingly clear that the heart of Radical doctrine was libertarianism: the defense of the individual's right to protection against encroachment by society or the state. "I would prefer," wrote the Radicals' unofficial philosopher, who used the pen name "Alain," "that the citizen remain . . . inflexible in spirit, armed with mistrust, perpetually suspicious of the plans and the reasoning of his leaders." Clemenceau did not need Alain's teaching to shape his political philosophy: for him it was second nature to stand at the barricades against the manipulators of power.

Within the Radical group, Clemenceau quickly earned a reputation as a political loner and an "aginner"—a man whose ruthless attacks in Chamber debates brought down cabinets, who became one of the most feared duelists in public life, whose rude, abrasive ways grew worse as the years went by, so that if he was respected and feared, he was not loved. Only a handful of disciples could stand the way he treated even those close to him. On one occasion, accused by a right-wing deputy of shady financial dealings, he rose indignantly and called on all his friends to join him in protest by walking out of the Chamber; as he stalked out proudly, he was followed by one lone supporter.

Outwardly at least, he seemed to have sloughed off that early idealism that had led him to offer free medical care to the poor and to advocate social reforms. He indulged increasingly in savage epigrams about friends and enemies alike— especially about those whom he regarded contemptuously as starry-eyed do-gooders. Yet this cynical shell concealed, I think, a vulnerable, lonely man, a sentimentalist at heart, who thirsted for human relationships but through shyness or an exaggerated sensitivity had grown a protective carapace against the world. And in the process, most of the intense idealism within that shell had shriveled away until nothing was left but the indestructible core—that ferocious individualism and that passion for the abstraction "France" that would survive intact until the end.

It is hardly surprising that such a man would not be very effective in what someone called "the republic of pals," where compromise and intrigue were the order of the day. Once again, in 1893, Clemenceau's career came to an abrupt and seemingly irreversible end: he was beaten for reelection by a rival who accused him, without evidence, of taking under-the-table payments from the British. His parliamentary career broken, his newspaper on the rocks, abandoned by most of his few friends, he thought seriously of suicide. An acquaintance who happened by the entrance to his newspaper office found him locking up and about to emigrate to the United States. This good Samaritan persuaded him to stay in Paris and provided him with an assignment as literary and artistic critic that would at least keep body and soul together.

In the same general election that cost Clemenceau his seat in parliament (1893), a new potential star won his way into the Chamber: Jean Jaurès. Younger than Clemenceau by eighteen years, Jaurès was a small-town boy from a respectable lower bourgeois family in the south of France. Jaurès was raised in genteel poverty. His father, a born loser, tried several different careers and failed in all of them. At the local lycée Jean proved to be a phenomenal student; he regularly won all the prizes. He was a dazzling talker as well. He walked alone in the woods, practicing speech making; sometimes the other young-sters, for want of entertainment, would persuade him to make extemporary speeches. His teenage ambition was a job in the local post office, but a visiting school inspector, struck by his talents, persuaded him to apply for a scholarship at the Ecole Normale Supérieure in Paris. Jaurès knew next to nothing about this *grande école*, or about its reputation as a training ground for France's intellectual elite. But he did apply and was accepted.

At Normale, Jaurès was again a brilliant success. Only one classmate could rival his brilliance: Henri Bergson, who was to become France's most eminent philosopher of his genera-tion. At graduation, members of the class were ranked in order; before the final oral examinations, bets were laid as to whether Bergson or Jaurès would emerge as number one. To everybody's consternation Jaurès was ranked third, Bergson second, and a certain Lesbazeilles first. The winner promptly vanished into permanent oblivion.

Jaurès returned to his home region to teach philosophy in the lycée at Albi, but soon moved up to a post at the University of Toulouse. In both roles he was a sensational success. His students later recalled that they had been virtually hypnotized by his rhetoric. Arriving in the classroom, Jaurès simply began to talk. Often the students suspected that he didn't remember what the topic was supposed to be, but they were nonetheless fascinated. Already, however, he was being attracted to poli-tics, for he was one of those reflective intellectuals with a strongly activist bent. He ran for parliament in 1885, and was elected—at age twenty-five, the youngest deputy in the Cham-ber. He sat with the group known as the Opportunists or Moderates, the party lately headed by the charismatic figure Léon Gambetta. But Jaurès's speeches in the Chamber upset his party colleagues, for he spoke of such things as social

Sketches of Jaurès as orator by A. Eloy-Vincent.

justice and the needs of the common man. In the 1889 elections the party leaders ran a strong candidate against him and sent Jaurès back to his classroom to meditate the risks of too much idealism.

Jaurès's exile, however, lasted for only four years. When he ran for parliament again, in 1893, it was under new colors, as an independent socialist. Jaurès came to socialism not through reading Marx's works (though he did read Marx and was influenced by what he found there). What drew him to socialism was his deep commitment to the concepts of brotherhood and justice: he was persuaded that since 1789 the Enlightenment current of liberal humanism had been steadily broadening and deepening and that socialism represented its logical culmination. Orthodox Marxists then and later were put off by what they saw as Jaurès's naive optimism about the fundamental goodness of man and the possibility of class collaboration. Clemenceau, one of his oratorical rivals in the Chamber, liked to gibe: "Do you know how to spot a speech by Jaurès? All the verbs are in the future tense."

It was tempting, of course, to caricature such a man. Politicians who stick to mundane matters and disabused realism are on safer ground. But Jaurès's florid style made things easier for his critics. Here, for example, is a passage from one of his typical newspaper articles of the time: "The triumph of socialism will make men understand the universe at last; they will see that it can't be brutal and blind. They will sense that there is spirit everywhere, soul everywhere, and that the universe is . . . an immense and confused aspiration toward order, beauty, freedom, and goodness." Such sentiments suggest that although Jaurès was outside the Church, he remained an essentially religious man. Indeed, he said frankly that he believed in God and that he was anticlerical only because the Church seemed always to be on the wrong side.

Jaurès's rhetoric might outrage both conformists and cynics, but it swept audiences off their feet. In the early 1890s he attended a socialist meeting in London, and forty years later one Englishman who was present still remembered the event vividly: Jaurès was young and little known abroad; he spoke in French, which almost none of his hearers understood; it was a hot August day, and the room was stifling. Yet he cast such a spell on these stolid Englishmen that at the end they were on their feet cheering, ready to march where Jaurès would lead them. Leon Trotsky, during his years of exile, used to go often to hear Jaurès and called him "the most powerful speaker of his time and perhaps of all times."

But Jaurès's impact was not solely the product of his rhetoric; rather, it was his whole personality that deeply impressed those who came in contact with him. Léon Blum, one of his disciples and eventual premier of France, wrote in retrospect: "There was a kind of saintliness about Jaurès. I mean by this a complete absence of personal motives: a purity of soul, a transparency of heart that was at times almost childlike. Never . . . were his thoughts and his actions distorted by any of those human motives that we find almost unconsciously within ourselves. He had no ambition, no vanity, no personal needs. Toward his enemies he was even more fair-minded than toward his friends." His was, perhaps, the naiveté of the child—or of the rare genius. He always expected the best of men and refused to lose faith even when they failed to measure up.

It would be hard to imagine a man more disorganized and absentminded, more indifferent to appearances. Jaurès went about in a chronic state of untidiness. If he wore a clean shirt it was because friends found one for him and suggested that he put it on. His wife early gave up, or lost interest. Often when he took the Paris bus from his home to his office, he found himself with no money for the fare; the conductor grew accustomed to stopping in at intervals to collect from his secretary. He was an omnivorous reader; he borrowed books by the hundred from every Paris library, and lost them by the dozen. Once, on a trip to the provinces, he was seen arriving at the station just as the train was about to pull out. In one hand he carried a battered valise hanging half open, revealing some odd articles of clothing and a hunk of bread and cheese; under the other arm was a pile of books that in the rush spilled all over the platform. A passing bourgeois lent a hand, before realizing that he had aided that dangerous radical Jaurès.

His appetite for the good things of life extended to the

pleasures of the table. When he visited peasant voters during his electoral campaigns, his hosts would bring out food and wine and would watch astounded as he wolfed down a hearty repast, sighing, "I really do enjoy these little snacks between meals." He always kept his intellectual interests, too. He was not only a voracious reader, but found time to write an eight-volume history of the Revolution (for which he was inspired, he said, by Marx and Michelet). Meanwhile he was also writing daily editorials in the socialist newspaper, managing the party organization, sitting and speaking in the Chamber, traveling incessantly around the country. His work load was incredible. After his death, friends planned an edition of his complete works but gave up when they found it would take some eighty or ninety volumes. For a man of disorganized habits, it was an impressive reckoning.

Jaurès's great achievement in politics was to bring together the fragmented socialist factions that had been wasting their strength in sectarian squabbles over doctrine or over leadership rivalries. The task took him ten years. He was hampered by divisive issues that kept intruding and by the suspicion among orthodox Marxists that he was not really a socialist at all. Was he, in fact, a socialist? Only in a broad and general sense. Jaurès read Marx *after* he began to call himself a socialist, not before. For Jaurès, Marxism was a method, not a dogma. For example, he accepted the premise that the economic factor is the mainspring of history, but he insisted that certain aspects of human life have a deeper source within the psyche: an innate urge for justice, a thirst for knowledge, a sense of beauty, a feeling of community with other men. He accepted the reality of the class struggle, but held that in the modern democratic state that struggle can take the form of peaceful competition. He accepted the necessity of revolution, but argued that it need not be bloody. Revolution to him meant a transformation of basic structures and values through legal processes, using the ballot instead of the bullet. In short, his was a socialism that sprang from the heart rather than from the head.

Rigidly orthodox Marxists were put off by this kind of value system and were further outraged by the fact that Jaurès refused to force his wife to give up her faithful practice of Catholicism. When word got out in 1901 that Jaurès's daughter was about to take her first Communion, some socialists demanded that he be expelled from the party. They set up an investigating committee that met sporadically for several weeks, harassing and insulting him. It was scandalous, one critic said, that a socialist leader should let his wife and daughter flaunt their superstition. "My friend," Jaurès answered mildly, "no doubt you can make your wife do whatever you wish. *Moi, pas!*"

Other issues too kept intervening to block Jaurès's effort at socialist unity. The most serious was the Dreyfus affair, involving an army officer, Captain Alfred Dreyfus, who was falsely accused of selling secrets to the Germans and was sent to Devil's Island for life. New evidence turned up that suggested Dreyfus's innocence, but army officials refused to reopen the case on grounds of national security. There were anti-Semitic overtones too; Dreyfus was Jewish. Most of the socialist leaders refused to join a crusade for a new trial, arguing that this was merely a squabble within the bourgeoisie. But Jaurès from an early stage plunged into the campaign. No socialist, he said, could be indifferent to flagrant injustice; human rights were not a matter of class but of fundamental principle. His was an unpopular position at the time; it contributed to his electoral defeat in 1898 (though he regained his seat in parliament four years later).

In 1905 he at last did achieve socialist unity. And by 1914, under his leadership, the party had become the second largest in the Chamber. But unity had its price. Jaurès was forced by the orthodox Marxists (notably the Germans in the Second International) to rule out socialist participation in any "bourgeois" cabinet. Without that proviso, Jaurès would probably have risen to a cabinet post in those prewar years—even, perhaps, to the premiership.

Meanwhile, what of Clemenceau? We left him in 1893 a beaten politician, abandoned by his friends, in debt, without prospects. He was to spend ten years in the political wilderness

Clémenceau.

Caricature of Clemenceau. Photo: Roger-Viollet.

before making his reentry into parliament. He survived during that time mainly through hack journalism. It was the Dreyfus affair that was to bring him back into prominence, for he was one of the very first to leap into the struggle for a new trial for Dreyfus. Some skeptics have charged that his real purpose in this crusade was to mount a political comeback. In fact, the Dreyfusard cause was intensely unpopular in those early years and hardly the vehicle for achieving political success. As with Jaurès, Clemenceau saw it as a matter of principle to stand up for any citizen, no matter how humble, when victimized by the institutions of society. Besides, "the Tiger" (a nickname in which Clemenceau rejoiced) liked a good fight against heavy odds. When, after a six-year struggle, the Dreyfusards finally won out, Clemenceau deserved and got a share of the credit. In 1903 he was elected to the Senate (which he had once wanted to abolish); two years later he achieved his first cabinet post, and in 1906, the premiership.

Clemenceau took power at a time of rising international tension and domestic social stress. He quickly showed himself to be a tough, uncompromising, even authoritarian leader. When massive strikes broke out, he mobilized troops to maintain order and described himself as "France's number one cop." He moved to counter the growing military power of Germany by building up the French forces and tightening France's alliances. His cabinet lasted for two and a half years, which was almost a record for the Third Republic. But when it fell, it seemed likely that Clemenceau would never again head a government. His policies had outraged most members of his own Radical party as well as the Socialists, yet he refused to throw in his lot with the conservatives because he doubted their loyalty to the republic and could not stomach their ties with the Church. Back he went to his isolated role as a political loner, increasingly crusty and abrasive, and stubbornly convinced that his beloved France now faced a mortal threat from the Kaiser's Germany.

Jaurès during this prewar decade had also been turning his attention to the war clouds building up in Europe. He threw himself into a study of national defense issues. He had opposed Clemenceau's strike-busting policies; this had led to a famous oratorical duel in the Chamber over the use of troops to repress the strikers. Jaurès, who had visited the strikers' homes in the mining towns of the north, declared himself appalled by the misery he had found there, and made a powerful appeal for social justice. Clemenceau replied, in typical fashion: "Monsieur Jaurès orates from great heights in creating his magnificent mirage, while I work down on the plain, on the hard earth which yields so little harvest." You, Clemenceau cried, have made the case for collectivism as the logical outgrowth of the French Revolution, while I have made my choice "*against* you and *for* the just and free development of the individual." Two forms of idealism thus met head-to-head; the issue between them was irreconcilable.

Jaurès also took a strong stand against the foreign-policy hawks, including Clemenceau. He was appalled by the arms race, which he saw as leading inevitably to war. His solution, after long thought, was a Swiss-style army of civilian militiamen—an armed citizenry ready to beat off invaders if necessary. And he advocated, if the governments of Europe did resort to war, a general strike by the workers of all the nations involved. This stance outraged the superpatriots of the right; they called him in print "a filthy prostitute paid by the Germans," or "the Kaiser's reptile." One journalist wrote: "If Jaurès were stood up against a wall and a good chunk of lead put where his brain is supposed to be, the firing squad would deserve congratulations." People mailed him parcels of garbage or human excrement.

In fact, Jaurès was not crusading for peace at any price, or for unilateral disarmament. Privately, he was disturbed at what he called "the brutality and hypocrisy" of the German leadership and was not at all sure that the German workers would heed a call to strike against war. But he sensed what kind of war this one would be, and he was convinced that every possible effort must be made to avert it. The fanatical nationalists, however, were not aware of his private views and continued to blast him in their newspapers as a traitor.

Out in the provincial city of Reims, these rabid newspapers

were being read by a young man named Raoul Villain. Nothing distinguished him except his insignificance: an obscure and colorless figure, he had failed his examinations at the end of lycée, and was drifting without job or prospects. On a brief visit to Paris he attended a performance of Corneille's *Le Cid* at the Comédie Française. This epic of a hero who single-handedly saved his country inspired him. Returning home, Villain got hold of two pistols, and scratched on their butts the names of Joseph Caillaux (a pacifist-leaning Radical) and Jean Jaurès.

July 1914 brought the international crisis that Jaurès had feared and foreseen. On June 28 a young Serb patriot had assassinated Franz Ferdinand, heir to the Austro-Hungarian throne, at Sarajevo. Three weeks of behind-the-scenes diplomatic activity followed before the Austrian government manufactured an excuse to declare war on Serbia. Now the great powers began to line up for the long-anticipated showdown. Jaurès threw himself with all his energy into heading off war, seeking to persuade the socialists of all countries to resist the hawks.

On July 31, Raoul Villain took the train to Paris and asked his way to Jaurès's newspaper office. Finding his quarry absent, he lurked about outside, trying to decide whether to wait longer or to return home. Jaurès meanwhile was at the premier's office, leading a Socialist delegation that urged calm and restraint. As they departed, the premier's aide asked, "What do you plan to do now?" "Carry on with our campaign against the war," answered Jaurès. "Look out," replied the aide, "you'll be assassinated at the first street corner." Jaurès shrugged off the warning and headed back to his office to write his editorial for the next day's edition. But first he joined some co-workers for a bite of supper at the Café du Croissant across the street. Villain saw them enter and asked a passerby to point out Jaurès. He approached the open window, next to which the Socialist leader was seated, and fired point-blank into his back . . .

Villain remained in prison for the duration of the war and was tried at last in 1919, in the euphoria of France's victory. Not even his lawyers questioned his guilt; they argued instead that this was the comprehensible action of a fervent young patriot seeking to protect his country against defeatists. He was promptly acquitted, and the trial costs were, in accordance with French procedure, assessed against Jaurès's widow. Villain vanished once more into the shadows until 1936 when, at his cottage in Majorca, he was gunned down by Spanish republicans who sought delayed justice for the murder of their martyred hero Jaurès. Meanwhile, in 1924, the parties of the left had returned to power in France, and in a great public ceremony had transferred Jaurès's body to the Pantheon.

What kind of editorial was Jaurès planning to write on the evening before war engulfed all of Europe? Did he intend to call on the workers to go on strike and refuse to be mobilized? Or would he have written an appeal for national unity, for the defense of the motherland against aggression? There is no way to tell, for Jaurès combined a hatred of war with a deep and genuine patriotism. We can only be sure of his long-term legacy to his countrymen, of which something will be said later. But first we must turn to the final phase in the life of his rival Clemenceau.

The outbreak of the First World War came as no surprise to the Tiger. He had been warning of the danger for years. And it opened the way for him to rise out of his obscure isolation into the spotlight once more. There is a curious parallel between his career and that of Winston Churchill: in both cases, decades of frustration and repeated failures, broken by a terrible national crisis that was made to order for such single-minded and pugnacious mavericks.

For the first three years of the Great War, as Frenchmen still call it, Clemenceau poured forth in his newspaper a stream of vitriolic criticism aimed at everyone in charge of the war effort, civilian leaders and general staff alike. Even more violent were his philippics against those defeatists who began after a time to urge a negotiated end to the war. By November 1917 the regime had used up most of its available leaders, and President Poincaré was faced with a harsh choice between Clemenceau and a defeatist such as Joseph Caillaux, who was known to favor a negotiated peace. With no hesitation but with great personal repugnance, he chose Clemenceau.

The Tiger threw himself at once into the task of winning the war. With Churchillian energy, he jailed or silenced the defeatists, replaced tired generals with aggressive types, squabbled with everybody because he wanted to run the war himself, but always backed off in the end rather than risk damage to the war effort. His leadership was undoubtedly an essential factor in the French victory (though whether in the long run that victory was better than a compromise peace—for France as well as for the world—may be open to debate).

When the great day of German surrender came on November 11, 1918, delirious crowds swarmed about in the street below his office, and friends and family gathered to share in savoring his great moment. But Clemenceau sat slumped on a sofa, gloomy and silent, refusing to go out to acknowledge the crowd's cheers. His daughter sought to dispel his mood: "Come, papa, tell me that you're happy." "I can't tell you what isn't true," was the moody reply. "It's all completely useless."

Thereafter, it was all downhill. Throughout the Paris peace conference, he was in sharp conflict with President Woodrow Wilson and Prime Minister David Lloyd George over treaty terms that would guarantee France's security against future German aggression; at the same time he faced the rising fury of the French hard-liners who complained that he was accepting far too many compromises. The hard-liners did their best to defeat the peace treaty when it came to parliament for ratification, and in 1920 they blocked Clemenceau's candidacy for the presidency of the republic as a final act of vengeance toward the man who, they said, had won the war but lost the victory. It was doubly ironic that after that burst of abuse from his own countrymen, it was the British and the Americans who became his bitterest critics—and for exactly the opposite reason.

The Anglo-Saxons branded him as the apostle of blind chauvinism, as the man whose purpose had been to destroy Germany. They ignored what he had said to the French parliament during the treaty debate: "Today, we are masters. Yet in the interests of our children and of the future, we must use our superiority with moderation. I don't want to run after the Germans' good will: I don't have the proper feelings for that. Still, sixty million people in the center of Europe will take some room, especially when they are men who have shown such brilliant qualities." They overlooked, too, what Clemenceau had said to his hard-line critics. Of course, he told them, this treaty has gaps and weaknesses; you can't write a perfect treaty or build a paper barrier against human conflict. One of my critics says, "Your treaty condemns France to eternal vigilance." Exactly so; "I see life as a perpetual conflict in war and in peace: that conflict you cannot suppress." The essential goal, Clemenceau believed, was to ensure that the wartime collaboration of France, Britain, and the United States be continued into the future, to guard against the resurgence of an aggressive challenge to the peace.

Clemenceau spent his last years in bitter retirement in his cottage in the Vendée, amusing visitors with cynical remarks about the politicians who had succeeded him in Paris ("a band of rats in a sewer"; "zero plus zero plus zero equals zero"). He emerged only once, in 1922, to embark on an unofficial goodwill visit to the United States, in a desperate effort to hold together the disintegrating wartime friendship. Almost everywhere he was greeted by enthusiastic crowds. At Yale, the undergraduates "cheered their lungs out"; in St. Louis, the Washington University beauty queen presented him with American Beauty roses and gave him a Southern smack on the lips. But there were some less agreeable moments also: violent attacks on French policy by Senator William E. Borah and Mayor "Big Bill" Thompson of Chicago, and a Harvard-Yale football game through which the Tiger was persuaded to sit (and which he described as a far worse ordeal than the Great War). On his departure, he donated the proceeds from his American speeches to the American Field Service for student exchanges between the two countries. But his tour had little effect in reversing American opinion, which was sliding fast into an anti-French and isolationist phase.

Clemenceau died in 1929 at age eighty-eight and was buried at the foot of a "tree of liberty" planted in 1848 by his father to celebrate the founding of the new republic. On his instruc-

Lloyd George, Orlando, Clemenceau, and Woodrow Wilson at President Wilson's residence in Paris.
Photo: Roger-Viollet.

tions, he was buried with a precious old book given him by his mother and a bunch of withered flowers presented to him in 1918 by soldiers at the front. At his request, there was no tombstone, and no priest. According to some reports, he was buried standing erect: even in death, it seems, the old Tiger would not lie down. His statue, which stands midway along the Champs-Elysées in Paris, was one of the few bronze statues spared by the German occupiers during the Second World War as they combed the city for metals to melt down for armaments. It was a mark of the Germans' respect for the tough old Jacobin; he had been a worthy enemy.

Any nation's schoolbook heroes are profoundly important in shaping that nation's values, the choices its citizens will make in times of both normalcy and crisis. A Jefferson or a Lincoln, viewed as a model, is likely to shape a cultural tradition that is quite different from one inspired by a Bismarck or a Napoleon, a Huey Long or a Richard Nixon.

Georges Clemenceau has become a French schoolbook hero: one sees his name enshrined on streets and squares all over France. He is a puzzling and contradictory kind of hero, admired not for his generosity of mind and nobility of spirit, or for his genuine and passionate libertarian defense of the individual's rights as against those of society and the state, but for his Jacobin spirit, his stiff-necked pugnacity in a time of grave national crisis. "He never became cynical about democracy," someone has written, "but only about those who practice it. He never became cynical about France, but only about Frenchmen."

Something more than that is surely needed for a healthy society, and it is important for France that alongside Clemenceau there is also a Jaurès whose influence persists. What Jaurès left as his legacy was a powerful myth, reinforced by his martyrdom at a most dramatic moment. He has become not merely a socialist hero, but part of the national heritage; for him, too, a street or square is named in most French cities and towns.

The eminent American political scientist James M. Burns has

reasserted, in his recent book *Leadership*, the importance of individual leaders to a nation's well-being, and has pleaded guilty on behalf of his profession to having underrated that importance by overrating power as the decisive factor in politics. Leadership, he argues, can take two forms: it can be "transactional" or "transforming." The former sort is more common; it involves skill at compromise, at horse trading. The second kind is more rare; through its exercise, "leaders and followers raise one another to higher levels of motivation and morality." Such leadership "raises the level of human conduct and ethical aspiration of both leader and led."

Jaurès, I believe, belongs in that pantheon of "transforming" leaders who can inspire not only their own countrymen but all men of goodwill. Toward the end of his life, with the European crisis looming, with Jaurès preoccupied day and night by that threat and by all of his manifold commitments, he still took time to participate in a university colloquium devoted to the work and influence of Leo Tolstoy. Jaurès wrote his own speech, and it ended thus: "In our narrow, confined existence, we tend to forget the essence of life. . . . All of us, whatever our occupation or class, are equally guilty: the employer is lost in the running of his business; the workers, sunk in the abyss of their misery, raise their heads only to cry out in protest; we, the politicians, are caught up in day-to-day battles and corridor intrigues. All of us forget that before all else we are men, ephemeral beings lost in this immense terror-ridden universe. We neglect the search for the real meaning of life; we ignore the real goals—serenity of the spirit and sublimity of the heart. To reach them—that is the revolution." Perhaps those words give final proof that Jaurès was not really a socialist. But they can surely stand as the epitaph of a great idealist, a great Frenchman, a great man.

Pierre Laval at his trial, October 1945. Photo: Keystone.

5

Three Episodes from the German Occupation: or, the Ambiguities of Treason

THE FUNCTION OF THE HISTORIAN, someone has said, is to conjure up the dramas of the past. Few historians today, however, would accept this function as anything more than a marginal one at best. Most of them would retort that their task is to look for meaning rather than drama and that the historian who lets himself be seduced by a taste for colorful episodes betrays his calling, for he is likely to slip into the role of mere storyteller or antiquarian. His rightful role, the professionals would argue, is to detect broader trends, to expose the deeper significance of human events, to measure the relative weights of change and continuity. Some of them would even contend that the historian should claim a place among the policy sciences and look for laws of development or even predict the future. They might even suggest that he should become a sociologist who finds his categories and builds his models in the past.

Yet, for some historians, sociology and predictive analysis

offer only partial satisfaction. Through the scaffolding of categories and strata and models, individual human beings stubbornly persist in poking their heads. True, these individuals often behave according to what one might call a kind of sociological law. They respond to the demands of their time, or their culture, or their class. But the fact that strikes the historian is the wide variety of individual human response to what would appear to be the same demands of time, culture, and class. Perhaps that variety of response is never greater than in a time of abnormal stress and crisis.

All of us are in varying degrees aware that we live in an age of moral ambiguity—an ambiguity greater than that faced by our ancestors or even our parents. Most of us, however, are insulated against these ambiguities by the routine nature of our daily lives. But sometimes a catastrophe such as war, defeat, or enemy occupation can strip away this comfortable insulation and can force men to face up to a set of painful dilemmas. Suddenly a man or woman may have to ask himself or herself, "Must I risk not only my own security but that of my family and friends as well, in the service of a higher principle?" Are there times when one must choose not between good and evil, but between a greater and a lesser evil? Have such traditional concepts as patriotism, loyalty, and treason become so cloudy as to lose their obvious meaning, so that at times the conduct that men normally call treasonable may become, in Raymond Aron's words, "the rarest and most sublime of actions, the last refuge of freedom"? Frenchmen after Hitler's conquest of their country in 1940 were forced to make some of these choices, and perhaps their diverse responses can tell us something about this unsettled age in which we all live.

It is true that for some Frenchmen the situation that followed the collapse of the French army and the armistice dictated by Hitler was clouded by no ambiguity whatsoever. There were those, for example, who at once rallied around Marshal Pétain, the national hero who headed the legitimate government at Vichy, while there were others who plunged at once into the resistance movement and never looked back. So it was with the writer Albert Camus, who was asked after the war why he had joined the underground, and replied: "It's a question that has no meaning for me; I simply couldn't conceive of anything else, that's all."

One example of such single-minded certainty may serve as a kind of backdrop to the three cases of ambiguity that will follow. Dr. Antonin Mans was a public health officer in the northern French city of Amiens. When the German armies rolled through Amiens in May 1940 and settled in to occupy the region, sealing it off from the rest of France, Dr. Mans stayed on at his post. A few weeks later, when the Vichy government asked him to assume even broader regional authority for public health matters, he took on those duties without question. But he accepted in order to carry on the war against the Germans. He organized a network of agents who would provide the British with detailed information about the German army's activity in this key region, at the narrowest point in the Channel.

In 1942 Dr. Mans took on an additional task. The Germans, finding themselves short of labor for their war industries, forced Vichy to agree to a labor draft of able-bodied young Frenchmen. Mans visited all of the doctors in his jurisdiction and persuaded them to furnish every young Frenchman with a certificate attesting to some sort of chronic ailment. When the German authorities grew suspicious, Mans offered to show them a sample of the available manpower. On the appointed day, some fifty young Frenchmen were assembled outside the local German headquarters—a collection of coughing, limping human wrecks. "You see, Colonel," the doctor explained, "it's just as Herr Hitler says: the poor French race has become completely degenerate." "Jawohl!" said the shocked colonel, "poor France!"

All went well until 1943. Then came disaster. One of the doctor's agents was caught by the Germans and forced to talk. Within an hour, Dr. Mans found himself in Amiens prison, already crowded with a mixture of resistance activists and ordinary offenders. As the Germans prepared the prisoners for shipment to concentration camp in Germany, some of

Mans's friends racked their brains for a way to free him. They turned to the Royal Air Force for help, proposing an air attack that would smash the prison gates and might permit the prisoners to escape in the confusion. The idea caught the RAF's fancy, and they carefully prepared "Operation Jericho." Using details smuggled out by the resisters, they built a small-scale model of the prison (preserved today in the Imperial War Museum in London) and made precise plans for a surprise low-level raid.

Precisely on schedule, the British planes roared over at rooftop height and smashed open the front of the prison. Dr. Mans's cell was also blasted open. He stumbled out, came upon a dead guard, seized his keys, and set to work opening the other cells. Then he headed for the exit, but as he ran, noticed some men who had been wounded in the bombing—including a German guard whose leg had been blown off. He stopped to administer first aid; and by the time he had cared for his patients, German reinforcements had arrived. He was seized and locked up again. The German prison commandant recommended to Berlin that Mans be freed as a reward for his heroism. But Berlin refused to let so dangerous an opponent go. A few days later, the doctor was packed into a cattle car for shipment to Buchenwald. Eleven months later, more dead than alive, he was liberated by the American forces, and returned to his public health job. He sought no honors or special favors; in his mind, why should he have done so? Had he not done the normal thing, as anyone in his position would have found it natural to do?

All of us, no doubt, would like to imagine that we would follow Dr. Mans's example in similar circumstances. But for some of the doctor's contemporaries, the choices were not so automatic and the responses were more problematical. Consider, for example, the case of René Hardy, who emerged from World War II a resistance hero, and then twice faced trial on charges of treason.

Hardy was a young civil engineer employed before the war on the French railways. Like Dr. Mans, he too was shaken by the French defeat of 1940 and set out to carry on the fight in his own way. Hardy's way was rail sabotage; his expertise permitted him to lay plans for disrupting the transportation system on which the German occupiers depended. So effective was he that by 1943 he was in charge of rail sabotage planning for all of France.

In June 1943 Hardy was summoned to a meeting of top-level resistance leaders in a suburb of Lyon called Caluire. The occasion was a visit by Charles de Gaulle's chief liaison agent with the resistance movements, an ex-prefect named Jean Moulin. The meeting was top secret. Only a few of the participants knew the exact location until a few minutes before the session began. The group gathered and had just begun its business when German Gestapo agents burst in, seized and handcuffed the lot, and carted them off to Gestapo headquarters in Lyon. There, Jean Moulin was so brutally interrogated that he died a day or so later, en route to a German concentration camp. As the chief martyr of the resistance, Moulin's body was transferred to the Pantheon after the liberation; he is the only Frenchman to be so enshrined since the war.

One participant in the Caluire meeting, however, escaped this brutal treatment. René Hardy was captured with the rest, but for some reason was not handcuffed. Outside, he broke away from his captors, leaped to the wheel of a Gestapo car, and roared off amid a hail of bullets. He made his escape, but one bullet winged him in the arm. Loss of blood forced him to abandon the car, and he was recaptured a few days later—this time by the Vichy police, who turned him over to the Germans. Again, his captors were surprisingly lax: instead of interrogating him they put his arm in a cast and locked him up in a military hospital in Lyon.

Meanwhile, French resistance leaders were badly shaken: how, they asked themselves, had the Gestapo learned of the secret rendezvous? The answer came promptly, and shook them even more profoundly. It came from a local Frenchwoman, a resistance activist who also worked for the Lyon Gestapo as a double agent. She reported to her underground contacts that the secret had been betrayed by René Hardy himself. It was a terrible accusation, but was it true? The double agent swore to its accuracy. She had been at Gestapo headquarters, she said, when Hardy informed the Germans of the Caluire meeting. But was a double agent to be trusted? To which side was she really loyal? If she had known of Hardy's betrayal, why had she failed to tip off the resistance leaders before the roundup? And why, after all, would the heroic young activist Hardy sell out to the enemy?

Finally, reluctantly, the resisters decided that they could not take a chance: if Hardy was suspect, better to liquidate him. They assigned that task to a woman who knew him, and who was to deliver a pot of poisoned jam to his hospital room. But again he was saved. When the woman arrived at the hospital she found that he had somehow escaped during the previous night and had vanished from sight. Before long Hardy turned up in Algiers and volunteered for de Gaulle's Free French forces. Some ugly rumors followed him, but he was accepted as a recruit, fought his way back into France in 1944 and then on into Germany, and emerged with a decoration for bravery under fire.

But Hardy's enjoyment of the hero's role was brief. When the Germans fled Lyon in August 1944, they left behind the local Gestapo files, and the French police went to work on them at once. There they found a damning document dating from 1943, two weeks before the Caluire roundup: it said that the Gestapo had received a tip about Hardy's rail sabotage activities, had followed him aboard a train headed for Paris, had arrested him en route, and had brought him back for questioning. Under threat of torture, the document stated, Hardy's nerve had broken. He had agreed to become a Gestapo informer.

It appeared to be a clear case. Hardy was arrested at once, and the press (with the Communist papers in the lead) understandably demanded quick and rough justice. Yet Hardy protested his innocence, and those who had known him well in the underground refused to believe the charges. France's most eminent criminal lawyer, Maurice Garçon, claimed to believe that a frame-up was involved, and offered to take Hardy's case. The trial came at last in 1947. In the courtroom, Hardy made an excellent impression. He seemed a clean-cut, straight-talking young man who exuded a sense of real integrity. It was true, he testified, that Gestapo agents had arrested him on the train; but when they had taken him off at a way station and were awaiting another train to take him back to Lyon, he had broken loose and made his getaway. Then why, he was asked, did the Gestapo report read otherwise? I have no idea, he answered; probably the officer in charge wanted to cover up his carelessness by making a false report to Berlin. The argument was plausible enough, even though not testable. Meanwhile the prosecutors bungled their case badly. Their only witnesses were sleazy types who had either been low-level Gestapo men or French double agents. It was Hardy's word against theirs. He was acquitted to the cheers of the courtroom crowd, and was wined and dined as a courageous patriot who had been vindicated at last.

Again, his triumph was brief. Two months later, the roof fell in. Someone who was searching through the railway records for the war years found the conductor's receipts for that Lyon-to-Paris trip in 1943; they contained the fateful notation: M. René Hardy, compartment X, arrested by Gestapo and taken off train at Chalon-sur-Saône, and returned to Lyon in custody. Confronted with this new evidence, Hardy wilted. He had indeed lied about his getaway. His captors did take him back to Lyon for grilling. But he had told them nothing, and after a day or two they had decided that they had arrested the wrong man. They had released him, and he had had no further dealings with the Gestapo until the roundup at Caluire. If this is true, the authorities asked, why did you tell that false story at your trial? If I had told the truth, he replied, who would have believed me? There were no witnesses to confirm the fact that the Gestapo released me and that I told them nothing. Why, then, they asked, did you not follow the unwritten rule of the underground and report your arrest at once to your resistance organization? You knew that the Germans sometimes released suspects in order to use them as decoys whom they could follow to the underground's secret hideouts. I thought of that, he answered, but it would have meant giving up my resistance activities, and I couldn't bear to abandon the fight to liberate France.

Few people were convinced. The Hardy legend collapsed. Almost everybody turned against him. From 1947 until 1950 he sat in a prison cell while the prosecutors prepared an airtight case. They tracked down the German who had headed the Gestapo unit in Lyon and got him to sign a deposition that Hardy had turned informer and had led them to the roundup scene. They dug into the central Gestapo files in Berlin, and found another report conveying the same information. They found Hardy's wartime mistress in Lyon and persuaded her to go state's evidence, testifying that he stopped coming home during the period just before the roundup and was spending his nights at Gestapo headquarters.

When Hardy was again led into court in 1950, he seemed a changed man. The old self-assurance was gone, and through the first few days of the trial the presumption of guilt piled up overwhelmingly against him. Yet toward the end, a shadow of doubt began to creep into the minds of many observers in the courtroom. There were his character witnesses—co-workers in the underground who had risen to high places in the postwar republic, and who swore to a belief in his integrity. There was Hardy's persuasive argument in his own behalf: why, if I sold out, was no one from my rail sabotage network arrested? I knew the hideouts of X, Y, and Z; why did the Gestapo let them run free?

The first turning point came when the prosecution called its star witness, Hardy's wartime girl friend Lydie Bastien. She went to the stand, said one journalist, "rolling her hips like a movie vamp"; and her act of betrayal of her former lover produced a wave of outrage among the male chauvinists present. Still more damaging were her responses to Hardy's direct questioning. She admitted that during his first stay in prison she had sent him food parcels and then, after his acquittal, had demanded payment for them. Worse yet, she confirmed the fact that she had sold to a tabloid the love letters he had written to her from his cell. At the end of her testimony, Hardy's lawyer shrewdly sensed the impact of the witness on the court; he turned his back, contemptuously refusing to cross-examine.

But lawyer Garçon saved his real trumps until the end: in

one dramatic summation, he managed to undermine the state's whole case. What he sought to do was to suggest that the prosecutors, in their indecent eagerness to get a conviction, had framed Hardy—that they had bought off a crew of German war criminals and French traitors to give false testimony in return for leniency. Virtually every item in evidence, he pointed out, had stemmed from one man—the ex-chief of the Lyon Gestapo, who had sent a written deposition rather than return to testify and be cross-examined. The documents in the Gestapo files had been written by him or his underlings, and their purpose was to conceal his own clumsy mistakes.

Suppose, argued Garçon, that it happened this way. The Gestapo did catch Hardy on the train and took him back to Lyon. But the obtuse Gestapo chief failed to realize what a big fish he had hooked; after a day or two, he let him go. Then, too late, he discovered his mistake, but Hardy could not be found. In panic, he tried to cover up by reporting to Berlin that Hardy had turned informer. Then, to his further embarrassment, Hardy was captured again at the Caluire roundup. What could he do with him? He could hardly grill and torture a man whom he had reported to Berlin as a valuable secret informer. But neither could he release him, knowing that he was a dedicated resistance leader. He hit, therefore, on a devilish scheme: he ordered one of his double agents to tell the resistance that Hardy had sold out, so that the resisters themselves would liquidate him. And his scheme barely missed succeeding; it was foiled only by Hardy's escape from hospital confinement.

It was an ingenious argument; and having made it, Garçon built up to an emotional climax. There on the witness bench, he cried, you see a motley crew of German war criminals and French traitors; here in the dock, one of the bravest of the freedom fighters. Today—May 8, 1950—is the fifth anniversary of Germany's defeat and France's resurrection. On this day of all days, will you let the Nazis win the last battle of the Second World War? There was furious applause, and when the panel of judges brought in a split-vote verdict of acquittal, there was a near riot of enthusiasm. Thus was René Hardy for the second time vindicated by French justice and proved a wronged and innocent hero.

Yet who besides Hardy himself and a handful of others really knows, or will ever know, what actually happened in Lyon in the summer of 1943? If he was really innocent, fate piled up an awesome collection of documentary and circumstantial evidence against him. At the very least, he was guilty of a terrible mistake in judgment when he concealed his arrest from his resistance colleagues: if he was released without any promises, the Gestapo no doubt trailed him to the Caluire rendezvous. At worst, he was a man who betrayed his comrades not by calculation but through weakness—through inability to face the kind of torture dealt out by the Gestapo. How great a crime is it to break under such pressure? How much courage do the rest of us (historians included) have a right to expect in this new medieval era of ours, with its brainwashing and terrorizing of prisoners? Questions such as these hung in the background during the trial, and may have shaped the outcome as much as the lawyer's clever tactics.

One of Hardy's character witnesses, the wartime air ace Pierre Clostermann, introduced these questions most effectively. Here is a man, said Clostermann, who in the teeth of a violent storm made his free choice to go out and face the elements, while most of his compatriots closed the shutters and waited for fair weather. He took upon himself the dangers of action, the risks of torture and death. Who among us— especially those who took the easy way—has a right to censure his passing weakness? Recently, added Clostermann, a British aircraft crew went on trial in London for having betrayed wartime secrets to the enemy. Shot down in 1944 by the Germans, threatened and manhandled by their captors, they ended by talking; thanks to what they said, the Germans a few days later shot down dozens of British planes in a single day. The facts of the case were clear; but when Air Marshal Sir Arthur Harris, wartime head of the RAF's Bomber Command, took the stand, the defense lawyer asked him one simple question: can you swear that you, in the same circumstances and under like pressures, would have kept silent? The hard-bitten old soldier looked hard at the lawyer and answered quietly, "No, I can't swear to it." The crew, like René Hardy, went free.

Alsace, as almost every schoolboy knows, is the province of France that borders on the Rhine and for centuries has been kicked back and forth like a soccer ball between the French and the Germans. Annexed by Germany in 1871, returned to France in 1918, ambiguity is built into its history and its very nature. If one had asked an Alsatian (until recently, at any rate) whether he thought of himself primarily as French or as German, he would probably have answered "Neither; I'm an Alsatian."

When Hitler's armies came smashing into Alsace in 1940, a good many Alsatians fled westward to escape the fighting. After the conquest was complete, Hitler denied most of them the right to return. He sealed off Alsace from the rest of France, placed it under the rule of a German *gauleiter*, and embarked on a propaganda campaign to convince the Alsatians that they belonged to the master race and would become part of Greater Germany for the next thousand years. Those who had escaped the invasion gradually scattered out through central and southern France, wherever they could find space to live and a way to survive. About a hundred of these refugees settled into a small village near Limoges called Oradour-sur-Glane, awaiting the time when they might return home. Oradour must have been a hospitable community, to take in so many wanderers.

Back in Alsace, some of those who had stayed behind were attracted by the Nazis' blandishments. But most of them did their best to ignore such talk and were content simply to live from day to day. With the passage of time, that grew more difficult. By 1942 Hitler was growing desperate for manpower for the new Russian front. He announced that young Alsatians would henceforth be conscripted into the German army. Some of the draftees resisted, took to the hills or escaped across the Swiss frontier. But this was terribly risky. If they were caught, they were shot; if they got away, their parents and families often paid the price by being rounded up and sent to concentration camps. Most young men were naturally encouraged by their parents to report for duty, and did so. During the next three years, one hundred thirty thousand young Alsatians were conscripted into the Nazi forces. Most of them were sent to the Russian front, from which half of them never returned.

A few of the draftees were luckier. They were sent to less dangerous duty in France, where their assignment was to guard the coasts against invasion and to patrol the back country against the *maquis* (the bands of French resisters who had taken to the hills and were engaged in guerrilla warfare against the occupiers). Some found themselves in the Waffen-SS division "Das Reich," posted to a relatively quiet area in southern France.

June 6, 1944—D day: the Allied armies land in force on the beaches of Normandy. Orders reach the "Das Reich" division to pack up and move north to Normandy at all speed. The troops are piled aboard trains and headed north, but now they face a new danger: the *maquisards* and "Fifis" (French Forces of the Interior, under de Gaulle's command) are emerging from their places of concealment, harassing the Germans, sniping and sabotaging. By June 9, "Das Reich" is still only halfway to Normandy. Near Limoges, the trains are stalled by a blown bridge. When an officer goes to investigate, he is picked off by a sniper in the woods.

The next day, June 10, is market day in the village of Oradour-sur-Glane, a few miles distant from the stalled division. Shortly after noon, the villagers are just getting up from a substantial lunch and the children are heading back to school when a convoy of trucks comes roaring into town carrying a company of 150 "Das Reich" soldiers. They quickly seal off all roads entering the village, then go through the streets rounding up everyone and herding them to the town square. Even the old and infirm are routed out, and the children marched over in a body from the school. Once assembled, the SS commander harangues the crowd. The villagers, he alleges, have harbored *maquisard* terrorists; the mayor must select and hand over thirty hostages as security against further attacks. The mayor, in an agonized reply, refuses to choose hostages, and offers himself and his family instead. The commandant angrily rejects the offer and barks an order. The women and children are lined up and marched off to the village church; the men are divided into smaller groups and herded into a half-dozen barns or cowsheds throughout town.

At the church, the troops carry in a heavy box with a long fuse attached; then machine gunners are posted at the doors and windows. A violent explosion rocks the building; the gunners open fire. When the screams inside have stopped, SS men bring in armloads of straw, pile up the pews, and set fire to the place. Meanwhile the explosion has served as a signal to the SS guards in the cowsheds; they open fire point-blank on their captives. Then through the late afternoon they rampage through the village, pillaging and burning, and at last pile back into their trucks and depart. A smaller detachment returns the next day, digs a common grave and throws in most of the bodies. By now the bridge is repaired, and "Das Reich" heads north again to join in the battle of Normandy.

When the French authorities in Limoges ventured out a few days later, they found 642 bodies at Oradour—half of them children, a third of them women. A handful of residents had miraculously escaped the slaughter: one woman somehow survived the church holocaust; five men shammed death in the cowsheds; one schoolboy took off through the fields, pursued like a rabbit by the German soldiers. Oradour became at once the representative symbol of German barbarism, the worst wartime atrocity committed in France. When the war ended a few months later, the French authorities naturally put top priority on finding these war criminals. After combing through the prisoner-of-war camps, they were able to identify some sixty men who had belonged to the killer company that devastated Oradour. In the process, they discovered a shocking fact: almost half of the culprits were not Germans but Frenchmen born and bred—young Alsatians in SS uniforms against their will.

A painful dilemma now confronted the French government. The nation would not let the government simply forget Oradour; but if it was to try these young Alsatians as war criminals, Alsace would explode. That province alone had been subjected to the German draft. Tens of thousands of young Alsatians had been killed in the fighting. It would be the last straw if some of the survivors were now victimized by French justice. Criminal charges would be sure to revive the old current of Alsatian separatism. It is hardly surprising that the government stalled. It quietly released the Alsatian prisoners and sent them back to their homes and families. Meanwhile it declared the ruins of Oradour to be a kind of national shrine and classed it as a historical monument to be preserved as it stood, a permanent memorial to Nazi barbarism.

The government hoped, of course, that tempers would cool and the whole thing blow over. It did not. Survivors and relatives of the Oradour victims pressed for vengeance. Most of the politicians from the Limoges region (the Communists especially) charged the government with engaging in a bourgeois cover-up. The government's hand was finally forced; in spite of furious protests in Alsace, it ordered a long-delayed court-martial.

The court convened in 1953, eight years after the massacre. In the dock were seven Germans and fourteen Alsatians. One by one, they were called to the bar and questioned by the judges about what they had seen and done in Oradour that day. They were hardly colorful witnesses. Almost all were village or farm boys who had been drafted at age seventeen or eighteen and who were more tongue-tied than eloquent. Each in turn claimed to be a victim of circumstance—conscripted by force, threatened by court-martial or death if he refused to obey orders. Most of them insisted that they had seen and done nothing; some said they had been assigned to guard the entrances and exits to the village and had not come into town at all. Those who were identified as having been at the church or in the execution squads claimed that they had faked obedience to orders by firing high, over their victims' heads.

Only two of the defendants stood out apart. One had welcomed the Nazis' arrival in 1940, had volunteered for the SS, and had risen to the rank of sergeant; all the other defendants charged him with responsibility for the Oradour atrocities, which he brazenly accepted. The second was a somewhat older man, now in his thirties, sad-faced and broken-spirited. He admitted frankly that he had been assigned to one of the execution squads and had then been ordered to the church to

Interior of the church at Oradour after the explosion and massacre.

help finish off the women and children. "Since that day," he told the court, "I've lost my peace of mind forever."

For the defense, both the lawyers and witnesses kept confronting the judges with one question: what would you gentlemen have done in their place? What can you expect of a teenager forced into uniform, knowing that his family will be victimized if he evades service? Can you really expect a young conscript to disobey an officer's order at the risk of being shot down like a dog? Is it not natural for every man to put his own survival first, at the expense of the lives of strangers?

For the prosecution, this was not an adequate excuse. No matter what the circumstances, it held, men are responsible for their actions: they do have a moral choice. They could have refused (as some others did) to put on a Nazi uniform, or to shoot people down in cold blood. By acting as they did, they betrayed their duty as patriotic Frenchmen as well as their obligations as moral men. Now, they must pay.

The judges' deliberation was long and evidently agonized. The verdict, when it came, was complex: for the German defendants and the one Alsatian sergeant—"guilty," with a sentence of death; for the others—"extenuating circumstances," with sentences of prison or forced labor varying from five to eight years. To the question "What would you have done?" the court thus answered with an implied assertion of belief in every man's free will and obligation to refuse to commit an inhuman act, no matter what the risks.

In Alsace, as expected, the verdict brought an explosion of fury. Bells tolled, public buildings were draped in black, protesters marched in the streets. The cry went up, "Every Alsatian has been dishonored." Meanwhile in the Oradour region there was equal fury. For 642 dead, a few short years in prison? In Limoges, fifty thousand angry citizens marched in protest; in dozens of villages roundabout, mayors and town councils resigned. The politicians in Paris, faced by a threat of civil dissension that might tear France apart, hastily sought a way out. A bill was rammed through parliament granting immediate amnesty to the convicted Alsatians. At first, this seemed to make things worse. The Alsatians called it an insult: their demand, they said, was for justice, not pity. In the new

Alsatian defendant in court at the Oradour massacre trial, 1953. Photo: Leonard McCombe. *Life* magazine,
© 1953 Time Inc.

village of Oradour, built a few hundred yards from the old, the town council removed from the city hall the Croix de Guerre, which had been awarded symbolically to the village, and put up at the entrance to town two blacklists—one bearing the names of the amnestied Alsatians, the other the names of the politicians who had voted the amnesty.

Gradually, however, things did settle down. The amnestied men were quietly conveyed in the dead of night from their prison back to their home villages, where they melted into their former obscurity. The Oradour authorities took down the blacklists—though not until twelve years had passed. National unity survived, but the affair left painful scars.

It left some painful ambiguities as well, unresolved to the present day. A tragedy of this sort involves both executioners and victims. But where does one draw the line between them? One ironic aspect of the whole affair was the presence of Alsatians on both sides. For among the 642 dead, about 60 were members of that Alsatian refugee group that had settled in Oradour in 1940. No doubt there were some young men among them who would have been conscripted, had they not been lucky enough to escape before the Germans arrived. They may even have been neighbors, schoolmates, of those who had become conscripted killers. Is it mere chance, then, that leads us to classify those on one side as victims, those on the other as executioners?

We may grant, too, that if the conscripts had refused to serve, or had disobeyed orders at Oradour, their persons or their memories would have been honored by Frenchmen and by historians for their courage and self-sacrifice. But does society (and do historians) have the right to expect such heroism of everyone? And if there is some reason to show compassion for these young Alsatian draftees, can we be much less compassionate toward the young Germans in that SS unit? Most of them were likewise drafted, and may have served just as reluctantly. Indeed, some of them may have come from the German province just across the Rhine, only a few miles from the homes of the Alsatians. Does moral responsibility, and associated guilt, depend on which bank of a river happens to have been one's birthplace? These are, fortunately, ambiguities that most of us will never have to face. Only if and when Oradour (or My Lai?) comes to Ohio, Texas, or California will we be forced, whether we like it or not, to choose and to judge.

The last of these case studies is probably the most ambiguous, complex, and paradoxical of the lot. For it concerns Pierre Laval, the number one villain of the war years in France—the man who served as Marshal Pétain's chief minister at Vichy in 1940 and again from 1942 to 1944, and who personified the policy of collaboration with the Germans.

To suggest any hint of ambiguity in Laval's case is likely to bring cries of outrage from most Frenchmen who lived through those occupation years. After all, Laval was tried and shot as a traitor after the liberation of France, and the standard image of the man still resembles what it was at the time. "An avowed Nazi-lover," says one American textbook; "an oily, unscrupulous political adventurer who represented fascism at its worst." Did Laval not tell his countrymen over the Vichy radio network in 1942, "I hope for a German victory, because otherwise the Bolsheviks will overrun Europe"? Did not his police help the Germans round up the Jews, and did not his government draft French workers to be sent to German factories? Indeed, did not his whole political career reflect a profoundly cynical opportunism, and did not his very appearance and manner— squat, swarthy, obsequious at times—suggest the inner nature of the man?

Laval's self-image was quite different. He remarked to a young Vichy official toward the end of the war: "I have no quarrel with the resistance people; you and I are resisters, too. For resistance you need two teams—one for offense, the other for defense." Laval insisted, and his friends have continued to insist ever since, that he consciously took on the most dangerous and ungrateful of tasks: to collaborate with the Germans in order to trick and befuddle them, thereby softening the impact of defeat on Frenchmen. Behind this facade, his partisans say, Laval played a masterly double game. Singlehanded, he reduced by a million the number of French workers

The Juggler. © 1940 Punch/Rothco.

shipped off to the German factories; by various dodges, he saved the lives of thousands of Jews and resisters; and he tricked Hitler into staying out of North Africa in 1940, when its conquest would have been easy and might have ensured Germany's victory in the Second World War.

Laval convinced himself that without his clever machinations France would have been given the Polish treatment—saddled, like Poland, with a Nazi viceroy, stripped of resources and manpower, bled white. He claimed in self-justification that he consciously faced the risk of martyrdom and the penalties of being misunderstood. "I don't know if I can pull it off," he remarked privately in 1943. "If I do, there won't be enough stones in France to put up statues of me. If I don't, I'll be shot, but that doesn't bother me—I will have done it for my country." Even more in character was his brusque rebuke to a friend who criticized his actions: "I'm up to my a-- in s---, for God's sake don't splash."

There is a good deal to be said for Laval's case. He was not the only statesman in history who had to make the best of a crushing defeat by collaborating with the conqueror. Some of these we regard as admirable men: Konrad Adenauer, for example, and Robert E. Lee. It is true, of course, that collaboration with the Nazis is not quite on a par with the choices made by Adenauer and Lee. It is true also that at the very outset, in 1940, Laval said publicly—and doubtless believed—that fascism was the wave of the future, and that Frenchmen had better get out their surfboards. But as the war dragged on, Laval apparently shifted to a policy of calculated duplicity, on the theory that he alone was clever enough to keep the Germans fooled. This was his conception of resistance—a natural conception for a man whose outlook was that of an operator, a fixer, convinced that human beings are on the whole weak and base creatures, and that the art of leadership consists of utilizing these baser instincts for some constructive purpose. His favorite epigram, after all, was said to be borrowed from Arab wisdom: "If you can't kill your enemy, give him your daughter in marriage."

It may be that Laval was right about human nature and the need to manipulate men rather than lead them. Perhaps there are times in a nation's history when calculated duplicity is the only remaining weapon. Perhaps there are moments when the only realistic choice is not the clear and easy one between good and evil, but the more ambiguous one between a greater and a lesser evil. This, at any rate, was Laval's conviction: that it was a lesser evil to order ten French hostages shot by the Vichy police than to stand aside while the Germans shot a hundred; that it was a lesser evil to turn all foreign-born Jews in France over to Hitler's tender mercies if he could thereby save most of the French-born Jews; that it was a lesser evil to round up a half-million forced laborers for German factories if by so doing he could prevent the roundup of two million more.

Laval's failing was to let himself slip much too far down the greasy slope of compromise with principle. At times he came to resemble the eighteenth-century politician Sir Boyle Roche, who is said to have declared in the Irish parliament: "Mr. Speaker, I should be prepared to sacrifice not only a part of our glorious constitution but, if necessary, the whole of it—in order to preserve the remainder." And Laval forgot, too, that in the process of misleading the Germans he might mislead and divide Frenchmen as well.

Whatever the verdict of posterity on Laval—and it is likely to be mixed—he probably meant well, had a clear conscience, and never regretted his actions. A true opportunist would have seen the way things were going, and halfway through the war would have found a way to switch sides, as so many did. Instead, Laval persisted doggedly to the bitter end, and faced his judges in the postwar courtroom with courage—or perhaps bravado. All of this may suggest that he had more in common with the stubborn, single-minded resisters like Dr. Antonin Mans than with waverers like René Hardy.

From these case studies in ambiguity, can one draw any conclusions about crisis behavior in our time, about the special nature of moral dilemmas in a secular and relativistic age, about the boundary line between patriotism and treason? A social scientist would no doubt try to find some sort of model that would establish categories and would have predictive value. A moralist would try to find in the wreckage of old standards and values some piece of intact furniture, a base on which to reconstruct firm moral judgments. Historians, unfortunately, are more likely to wallow in these moral dilemmas, and to plead that their task is to understand rather than to judge. They would not be very helpful, therefore, if Americans were suddenly faced by the kind of choices that Frenchmen confronted after 1940.

Still, perhaps the historian can observe that these case studies suggest what one might call a temperamental interpretation of history: that one can rarely predict, on the basis of some statistical analysis, or class origin, or age or condition, how individual human beings are going to behave in crisis circumstances. In our age, as in any age, crisis behavior is likely to spring from impulses deep in the personality structure or even the subconscious, impulses that combine differently from one individual to the next.

Indeed, it is tempting to think that in our age of mass society and the so-called mass man, when the individual allegedly no longer counts, these differences of character may be even sharper than in times past; for in the past the individual's conduct was more completely bounded by the context of family, community, culture, and nation. That context, that protective envelope, narrowed the alternatives before a man or woman, and made his or her responses more automatic. But in our day the lonely individual, partially freed from those confines, is left to seek deep within himself the springs of decision and responsibility. And in the divergent responses of individual men and women to crisis one may find—as an ancient moralist once put it—"all the deep and twisted complexities of the human heart, deceitful above all things."

Photo: Imperial War Museum.

6

Echoes of Cincinnatus: or, de Gaulle in History

THERE IS A STORY, very possibly apocryphal, to the effect that on the morrow of the death of the novelist François Mauriac, President Charles de Gaulle spoke feelingly of this eminent writer at a cabinet meeting, and ended by describing him as "the greatest master of French prose of our time." Then, noting the presence at the table of his Minister of Culture André Malraux, he is supposed to have added, "among others."

No one, eulogizing Charles de Gaulle in the presence of all other French politicians and statesmen of his time, would have had reason to look about and to add "among others." As de Gaulle stood out physically in a French crowd because of his height, so he stood out dramatically above the rest in the congregation of his contemporaries who played public roles. Such men are likely to cast long historical shadows—though posterity, and the historians, sometimes fail to do them justice. What the future will say about Charles de Gaulle may still be problematical; but for de Gaulle himself, it was not a matter of indifference. For him, history was serious business. And though barely a decade has passed since his death, it is already natural to speak of him in the context of history.

Except in his most pessimistic moods, Charles de Gaulle believed strongly that men *can*—both as individuals and in groups—shape their own history. As a young instructor of history at the military academy of St. Cyr, he used to tell the cadets: "Get this lesson into your heads: history doesn't teach fatalism. Fatalism is only for cowards. There are times when the will of a few men shatters determinism and opens up new paths." And again: "People have the history they deserve."

He rejected fatalism, yet believed, paradoxically, in the operation of destiny: certain individuals and nations were singled out for greatness. "France is not really herself," he wrote at the outset of his memoirs, "unless she is in the front rank." During his year at the War College in Paris in the mid-1920s, a fellow student remarked, "Somehow I have a strange feeling that you have a great destiny before you." *"Oui,"* replied de Gaulle soberly, *"moi aussi."* In London during the war, he confided to a young disciple, Elisabeth de Miribel, that at age twelve he had come to realize that some mysterious force had marked him out to lead France in a future moment of crisis. He had therefore abandoned childish pleasures and had laid out for himself a program of rigorous reading in history, geography, philosophy, and the classics to prepare for the day. He startled one English acquaintance in 1941 by remarking: "Every day I take a little time off to examine my role in history."

History for de Gaulle was rich in meaning; indeed, he liked to spell it with a capital *H*. This was not mere professional bias, stemming from the fact that both he at St. Cyr and his father at a Catholic secondary school had been teachers of history. Rather, it was because he saw in history the key to understanding the present: man's role, and man's potential. The record of the past, for him, did not show a pattern of gradual upward progress toward some ultimate utopian age, as the Enlightenment thinkers and Hegel (and Marx, in his own fashion) believed. Instead, it was marked by irregularity and uncertainty; it was a kind of heroic adventure in technicolor, in which chance was always operating, and in which the leading roles were entrusted to a few exceptional individuals and to one privileged nation. Some critics—including Franklin Roosevelt and Winston Churchill—accused him of suffering from historical delusions, identifying himself with Napoleon or Joan of Arc. The truth, one biographer observes, is simpler: it resembles the well-known sardonic remark about Victor Hugo as *"un fou qui se croyait Victor Hugo."* Charles de Gaulle simply took himself for Charles de Gaulle.

The man Charles de Gaulle was born in Lille in 1890, the son of a conservative Catholic teacher, the descendant of lesser aristocratic stock. His father's value system had its paradoxical side. Although solidly right wing, he belonged to that category of fervent believers known as "social Catholics," who accepted a paternalistic responsibility to improve the lot of the lower orders. Even more unorthodox was the elder de Gaulle's support of Dreyfus during the great turn-of-the-century crisis that pitted justice for the individual against the authority of the state. These contradictory traits, in somewhat different form, were to recur in the son.

But the historical personage General de Gaulle, he tells us in his memoirs, was born fifty years later, in 1940. He recalled discovering, soon after he went to London, that "there existed in people's minds someone named de Gaulle, with a personality separate from my own. From that day forward . . . I became almost the prisoner of [this historical de Gaulle]. Before every speech and decision I asked myself: is this the way people expect de Gaulle to act? Many things I should have liked to do but did not do because they were not what was expected of General de Gaulle." So in his memoirs he switches back and forth between the first and the third person as he speaks of the two de Gaulles. To some degree, of course, most men in public life find their real selves displaced by their public images. But rarely has this been so flagrantly true as in de Gaulle's case, and almost never has it been so self-conscious. The effect, Alfred Grosser has said, is that he lived not so much his own life as his own biography—that he behaved according to what he wanted history to say, and consciously created a legend for future historians to use. His memoirs were clearly written with this in mind.

Few men who achieve greatness have come to public notice so late in life. He was already forty-nine when he broadcast his famous appeal to his countrymen from London, proclaiming that France had lost a battle but had not lost the war. Until then, obscurity and frustration had been his lot. During the Great War he was wounded in action and captured by the Germans; he fretted away two years as a prisoner of war. Afterward, he developed a reputation as a military maverick. At the War College, where he challenged official doctrine and argued with the professors, the faculty voted to rank him in the lowest third of the graduating class—which would have ended his military career. He was saved by a marshal who had taken him on as a kind of protégé—Philippe Pétain. Thereafter, he wrote books on military leadership and strategy that were not much appreciated by the top brass; one of them led to a falling out with Pétain. By 1939, he was only a colonel of infantry.

Read in retrospect, these books of the interwar years were both significant and revealing; they not only advocated a new kind of mechanized army, but called for a new sort of military leadership. De Gaulle deprecated the kind of officers that had risen to the top after 1918: cautious, defensive, routine-minded types. Men must be led, he wrote, as they must eat and drink; they will turn in time of stress to the man of character. Such a leader is likely to embody "a strong element of egoism, pride, toughness, cunning." He will consciously build up his prestige by creating an aura of mystery, through an aloof demeanor and a sparing use of words and gestures. Subordinates, mediocrities for the most part, will complain that he is rude and demanding; but let the crisis come and all is forgotten. "A sort of ground swell brings to the forefront the man of character. All that he asks is granted." It was a remarkable self-portrait, accurately anticipating the "historical" de Gaulle.

Chance, or fate, brought him out of obscurity in June 1940. Shortly before the Germans attacked France in May, de Gaulle had been named a two-star general and given command of a newly organized armored division. He acquitted himself brilliantly during the Battle of France, and was called to Paris early in June to become undersecretary of war. But the French armies were disintegrating, and when the cabinet voted to capitulate, de Gaulle refused to conform. On June 17 he took "French leave" (the French, paradoxically, call it *"filer à l'anglaise"*—i.e., taking English leave); he hitched a ride to London with Churchill's special representative in France. There, the next day, he made his famous radio appeal to Frenchmen to continue the fight against Hitler, and waited for some major political or military figure to speak out.

De Gaulle was ready to serve under such a leader, but when none turned up, he stepped into the vacuum. Clearly he was not reluctant; probably he was not surprised. A lesser man might have become just another refugee soldier volunteering to fight in the British army; many Poles, Belgians, and Dutchmen did just that. His ambitions were higher. He was convinced that France was different from the other conquered nations and that someone had to speak for France in Allied councils. Anthony Eden, Britain's foreign secretary during the war, said to him after the war ended, "Do you know that you caused us more trouble than all the other Allies put together?" "I don't doubt it," de Gaulle replied; "France is a great power." Such a belief at the time seemed absurd. France in 1940 had never looked less like a great power.

Frenchmen like Jean Monnet, head of the French purchasing mission in London and later to be known as father of the European Common Market, urged him from the start to forget the idea of setting up a government-in-exile in London. It would, said Monnet, inevitably be regarded as a British puppet and would carry no weight in postwar France. De Gaulle shrugged off the warnings and foiled the critics. By 1944 he was recognized as the unquestioned leader of liberated France, with a clear mandate to take control in his badly shattered country. Through the war years his sensitivity to real or fancied slights, his lofty insistence on France's right to be treated as an equal in Allied councils, had annoyed Churchill and exasperated Roosevelt. Churchill complained that the Cross of Lorraine (the Free French symbol) was the heaviest cross he had to bear, while Roosevelt vented his anger in private jokes about de Gaulle's alleged megalomania and dictatorial ambitions. In a sense, these Anglo-Saxon attitudes played into de Gaulle's hands; they neutralized any French suspicion that he might have become a British cat's-paw. At any rate, he returned to France shortly after D day, a legendary figure; thousands of Frenchmen had heard his voice, but almost none had seen him in the flesh. Rarely in modern history has a man so little known to his countrymen taken power in a major nation (though Americans in recent years have gained some experience in being governed by unknowns).

How should one judge this first chapter in the career of the "historical" de Gaulle, as exiled leader of France in London and then in Algiers? Some skeptics think that it would not have made much difference if de Gaulle had failed in his escape to London in 1940; some other figure, they argue, would have emerged to lead Free France and to weld together the exiles and the underground. Perhaps so. But it is by no means certain that a less stiff-necked leader could have avoided the appearance of being an Anglo-American agent, or that a less forceful figure could have managed to fuse together the fragmented underground forces in France into a national resistance movement. It may be, too, that another leader might have failed to prevent the Communists from emerging with a stranglehold on the entire resistance movement. That party's real goals during the war and the liberation period are still controversial matters today. Perhaps the Communists hoped to seize control outright, or, more probably, they may have been thinking of a more gradual route to power, winning enough key posts in the government to permit a gradual takeover on the Czecho-slovak model. De Gaulle, at any rate, believed that their goal was not mere liberation but power, and set out to prevent it. Well before D day, through toughness and charisma, he managed to impose his authority on the reluctant Communists in the underground.

Back in France, de Gaulle found the resistance forces engaged not only in helping to fight the Germans but also in administering rough justice to all those suspected of Vichyite

De Gaulle's grand descent on the Champs-Elysées, August 26, 1944. Photo: Keystone.

sympathies. From the outset, his public stance was that all but a handful of Frenchmen had been resisters, so that few needed to be punished. This was hardly true: most Frenchmen had been *attentistes,* inactive observers of the Franco-French war between collaborationists and resisters. But it was a useful fiction that permitted the deep divisions among Frenchmen to be healed, or at least patched over. It reduced the danger of civil war during the liberation period and the threat that the Anglo-Saxons might impose a military occupation regime to restore order.

This second chapter in de Gaulle's career was to be short; he served sixteen months as provisional president of the republic or, one might say, dictator by consent. Judging his success during this period is more difficult than in the case of his wartime role. At the outset, he seemed to enjoy a great opportunity to renovate France from top to bottom. Most Frenchmen claimed to want drastic change; and the old vested interests, tarred by the Vichy brush, were temporarily chastened. Some things *were* accomplished in those sixteen months, but far less than the reformers had hoped. The facade of national unity was soon broken. There was a return to political squabbling and to a weak, unstable governmental system. And the regime missed its chance to liberate the colonial empire by gradual stages, without the bloodshed that was to mar decolonization in Vietnam and Algeria.

How much of the blame should be assessed against de Gaulle? No one, probably, could have done all that was wanted and needed at the time. But it is clear that his rigid and authoritarian manner offended many politicians and aroused suspicions about his real aims. Was he truly committed to democratic processes and values? The critics pointed out that he had at one time been an admirer of the right-wing neomonarchist Charles Maurras; they wondered if he had really changed. Léon Blum, the Socialist leader, was inspired to remark that de Gaulle "stands for democracy but does not embody it."

When de Gaulle brusquely announced his resignation as provisional president in January 1946, declaring cryptically that he had completed his work, the nation and the politicians were stunned. Years later, it became known that he intended this action to serve as a psychological shock that would bring the squabbling parties together, force their leaders to plead with him to return, and give him authority to dictate a restructuring of the republican system. He retired to a forest retreat near Paris, and waited for the delegations of supplicants to appear. None came. At last he sent an aide into the city to see whether the police had barricaded the exits against the delegations; the aide returned to report that all was quiet. Bitterly disappointed, de Gaulle departed for his country retreat in the tiny village of Colombey-les-Deux-Eglises, there to begin a twelve-year self-exile later described by his disciples as "the crossing of the desert."

The metahistorian Arnold Toynbee, in his massive *Study of History*, tells us that the careers of great men are normally marked by phases of "withdrawal and return." Abandoning the poisons and delights of power, by choice or by necessity, they retreat to some isolated spot, engage in reflection and renewal of spirit, and regain the aura of transcendency that may have become a bit tarnished. They are ready then to return to greatness.

This phase of de Gaulle's career does not quite fit that ideal pattern. It has a certain fascination, but does not show the man at his best; frustration brought out the petty streak that often dwells in great men. He displayed the reflex of one who sees his destiny snatched away, not by powerful rivals but by pygmies. He spent his energies railing against the new Fourth Republic and the politicians who managed it; "scum floating on the ocean" was one of his typical epithets. For a time, he sponsored a Gaullist party committed to the idea of ridding France of the flabby new regime. The party scored a remarkable electoral success in 1951, but when some of its leaders were co-opted into accepting cabinet posts, he angrily washed his hands of the operation and turned to writing his memoirs.

Visitors who came to Colombey from time to time gave contradictory reports of this giant brooding in exile, torn between a belief that destiny would call him again and a desperate fear that age was catching up with him, that history

De Gaulle in Algeria, June 1958: *"Je vous ai compris."* Photo: Keystone.

had passed him by. One visitor, a few months before the Algerian crisis of 1958 that was to bring him back to power, heard him sketch out a scenario that foreshadowed almost exactly what was about to happen. But another interviewer, an American in this instance, found him in a state of deep dejection. "Ah, poor France!" went de Gaulle's gloomy soliloquy; "France is finished for good. Oh, perhaps somebody might discover on French soil some rare mineral that would transform the world balance; but unless that happens, there's no hope." Some of his loyal disciples tried from 1956 on to involve him in active preparation of a coup d'état against the Fourth Republic, but he refused even to discuss it. At the same time, he would lend no moral support to the beleaguered republic, bogged down in the Algerian struggle and increasingly threatened by subversion. "Why give shots to a corpse?" he remarked acidly to a visitor.

The crisis came at last in May 1958. A new cabinet in Paris seemed inclined to negotiate an end to the war in Algeria, and this threat led to violent action by the die-hard settlers in Algiers, supported by part of the army officer corps. The protesters on May 13 seized control of the city of Algiers, and for a time there were reports that they might mount a paratroop drop on Paris to impose some kind of military regime. De Gaulle played his cards shrewdly; he had learned something from his first spell in power. He declared himself ready to serve if called; he negotiated with both the politicians and the army leaders, handling them with skill and finesse. By the end of May, most of the leading politicians had decided that de Gaulle alone could save them from rule by a military junta, while the settlers and the army believed that he would serve their interests by keeping Algeria French. On June 1 parliament endorsed de Gaulle as premier, with a grant of full powers to resolve the crisis. Parliament was suspended for six months, and the Fourth Republic shortly gave way to the Fifth.

In office once more, one of de Gaulle's immediate concerns was his age. "I arrive ten years too late," the then sixty-seven-year-old de Gaulle told his doctor fretfully. "Ah, if I were only sure of having ten more years before me." In fact, he had twelve years—eleven of them in power. A quick trip to Algiers in June won the support of the European settlers there; *"je vous ai compris,"* de Gaulle told the cheering crowd (whose members later wondered if the phrase had meant, instead of "I understand your feelings," "I've got your number"). Back in Paris, he handpicked a committee to draft a new constitution on purely Gaullist lines; it provided for a strong executive and a drastically weakened parliament. He was promptly elected president of the new Fifth Republic for a seven-year term and chose one of his most fervent supporters, Michel Debré, to be prime minister, authorized to run all aspects of government that did not seriously interest de Gaulle himself.

In his own sphere of action, ending the war in Algeria took top priority. Yet achieving that goal took four long years. Why so long? De Gaulle was to assert in his later memoirs that from the very outset he knew that Algerian independence was unavoidable, but that Frenchmen generally were less farsighted, so that time was needed to bring them around. Furthermore, he recalled, he had been determined not to preside over a French defeat; he intended to carry on the fight until Algerian independence might come as a gift from France. If he was being candid, those four years of bloody combat constituted a heavy price to pay for saving face. He was probably not completely candid; for the first year or two, it seems most likely that he still hoped for a compromise arrangement that would stop short of independence and would maintain an ongoing special relationship between Algeria and France.

In the end, however, he faced up to necessity and made a virtue of it. In March 1962 he negotiated disengagement on compromise terms that gave Algeria true independence. Meanwhile, the vast expanse of Black Africa had broken away also. Again, de Gaulle accepted the loss philosophically, and even offered to aid the ex-colonial territories by providing them grants and by sending technical experts. His realism paid off; French influence remained strong in the new African states, and de Gaulle's personal prestige there rose to new heights.

Disengagement nevertheless had its costs; it brought on a year or two of tension and violence that seriously threatened to mushroom into civil war in France. A segment of the army in Algeria, including some top generals, formed a subversive movement called the *Organisation armée secrète* (OAS), which embarked on a last-ditch effort to keep Algeria French. Through 1961 and the early months of 1962 OAS terrorists carried out daily bombings and assassinations in the Algerian cities and in Paris as well. Several attempts were made to assassinate de Gaulle; on one occasion his car was caught in a cross fire, and one bullet missed him by only two inches. Toward the end, the OAS and its allies among the European settlers turned in desperation to a scorched-earth policy of sheer destruction. After this bloody last hurrah, the panic-stricken settlers swarmed aboard ships and planes sent to evacuate them to safety in France; more than seven hundred thousand of them were jammed into refugee camps in the Marseille region, awaiting the massive task of resettlement. It is hardly surprising that this *Götterdämmerung* left some deep scars; what is more surprising is that most Frenchmen quickly absorbed and forgot the loss of Algeria. Luckily, the economic boom of the 1960s eased the problems of resettlement and adaptation, and kept Frenchmen's energies occupied. Yet the crisis of disengagement from Algeria had brought France perilously close to civil war, and there is reason to doubt that anyone lacking de Gaulle's stature and nerve could have successfully led the country through that crisis.

This problem solved, de Gaulle now faced a new confrontation: this time with the politicians. Since 1958 they had been chafing at their reduced role, but they had dared not challenge the president so long as the Algerian war continued. Once it was over, they moved to clip his wings by revising the constitution to restore parliament's authority and to reduce presidential power. But de Gaulle beat them to the draw, announcing his own proposal for constitutional amendment that went in precisely the opposite direction. The president, under this proposal, would be chosen by direct popular election rather than by a college of notables. This was sure to reinforce presidential authority, since no other official could claim to be the choice of the whole nation. In the referendum that followed, the amendment was bitterly opposed by most of the politicians and the press; and in the end, it was approved by only a sixty-two to thirty-eight margin. For de Gaulle, this was almost a defeat.

Bitter and disillusioned, he seriously considered resigning once more. "The French are cattle," he fumed privately: "incapable of discipline. After me, they'll slide back into chaos." But he quickly shook off his disappointment, and was reassured by the nation's response to a new political party, the Union for a New Republic (UNR), organized by his disciples and committed, it was said, to a one-plank platform: *"de Gaulle, oui!"* The UNR won a sweeping victory in the parliamentary elections of November 1962, thus ensuring de Gaulle's new regime against successful challenge.

Now came the golden years of the mid-1960s—years of unbroken stability and success. More and more, the president's role resembled that of an elective monarch surrounded by his admiring courtiers, and receiving the visits of world statesmen who flocked to Paris: from Khrushchev and Kennedy to the new African presidents, arriving seriatim. It was a time of booming prosperity; the gross national product rose at an unprecedented rate, outpacing that of most other European nations. France was clearly being transformed into a modern, efficient industrial state.

Legends clustered around the aging sovereign, suggesting that he identified himself with France. Pursuing the Germans across France in 1944, according to one apocryphal story, an aide reminded him that they were passing near the birthplace of Joan of Arc and suggested that he detour slightly to visit the shrine. "Yes, I'll go," he is supposed to have answered; "she deserves it." An aide is alleged to have declared, "For twenty years I've been saying that Germany is a constant threat to France"; to which de Gaulle replied, "I, de Gaulle, have been saying it for a thousand years." A cartoonist depicted the president and his wife reading in bed as the radio signed off with the "Marseillaise"; Madame de Gaulle turned to her husband with "Oh, Charles, our song!"

This lofty position naturally had its costs: especially a sense

De Gaulle with President John F. Kennedy. Photo: Dalmas.

of isolation, and the strain of having always to play the public role of General de Gaulle. At times, he remarked to a confidant, he wished that he could occasionally be plain Charles de Gaulle, strolling down the Champs-Elysées or riding the Métro like an ordinary Parisian. He gave up cigarettes because someone persuaded him that they affected his eyesight; when abstention failed to help, he itched to light up again but resisted the urge because, he said, it would be a sign of weakness and people would not understand such weakness in de Gaulle. He refused to receive telephone calls in person; he called it demeaning. An aide one day asked, "Do you recall the time when [X] was chatting with you about . . ."; de Gaulle interrupted testily, "One doesn't chat with General de Gaulle; one converses with General de Gaulle." His qualities did not include a capacity for warm human relations. Years earlier he had remarked, "A real leader can have no friends because he has no equals." In him there was no strain of humility and rarely a sign of compassionate understanding of lesser mortals. He once said, "My problem is that I respect only those who oppose me—and them I can't stand." If he demonstrated a certain arrogance, it was not an artificial trait but an integral part of the man.

For the outside world, for many Frenchmen, and probably for de Gaulle himself, the most important aspect of the Gaullist regime was its foreign policy. This branch of public affairs he reserved primarily for himself, whatever the constitution might say to the contrary. In his view, any nation in our time has only two choices: either to be an independent great power or to become a kind of satellite of one of the superpowers. For him, only the former choice could even be contemplated: "France cannot be France without greatness." Joined to that premise was a second basic assumption: that the primacy of the nation-state is a fact of life and that each nation, whatever its idealistic professions, looks out for its own interest. From these convictions sprang his policies on particular issues: his skeptical attitude toward European integration, his veto of Britain's entry into the Common Market, his rapprochement with France's longtime enemy Germany, his determination to develop nuclear weapons, his expulsion of NATO forces from

French soil, his denunciation of American intervention in Vietnam, his cry of "Free Quebec!" in a quixotic campaign on behalf of Canada's French-speaking province. As he once put it, "War is waged against one's enemies; peace is waged against one's friends." If he took what seemed to be an anti-American stance at times, it was because he viewed the United States as currently the world's most powerful nation, devoted like any other to the pursuit of its own interests. Its strength, de Gaulle believed, required France to deal with the Americans as the chief threat—for the time being at least—to French independence and to world peace. Any nation with excessive power, in his view, would be tempted to misuse it—the United States more than most, given its immaturity in world affairs.

De Gaulle's admirers, then and later, have argued that in all this he was generally right; that through his realistic understanding of the world in which we live, of the nature of power and the central role of the nation-state, he was on the side of history. For his critics, on the other hand, his policies undermined the solidarity of the Atlantic world and interrupted the process of European integration, which they saw as France's best bet for recovering leadership in Europe. On his side, it can be said that he rested his foreign policy on a clearly conceived world view and knew what he was after. He also gave his countrymen what most of them wanted: an expanded self-esteem, after a generation of hard knocks and defeats. Even the Communists dared not attack him on the foreign-policy front; and one strongly anti-Gaullist Socialist confessed with some embarrassment that when de Gaulle slammed the door of the Common Market on Britain, he "felt proud of being a Frenchman for the first time in my life." Why? "Because we finally stood up to somebody, and said 'No.' " Still, the popularity of a foreign-policy line is not necessarily the best test of its long-range soundness. We cannot yet be sure whether Gaullism was "on the side of history," or whether France and the world might be better off today if that policy had been less intransigent and "realistic."

Two episodes during the 1960s marred these triumphal

years. The first of these occurred in 1965, when de Gaulle's presidential term came to an end and he faced the choice of seeking reelection (at age seventy-five) or stepping down to well-earned retirement. De Gaulle had once criticized his former patron Marshal Pétain for hanging on too long: "Old age," he had remarked, "is a shipwreck; no man should let himself grow old in office." But he felt no impulse to follow his own advice, and so he offered himself for reelection. To his dismay, rivals emerged; the forces of the left resolved their differences and coalesced against him. He failed to get a clear majority on the first ballot, and won the runoff by only a fifty-five to forty-five margin. Although he grumbled for a time about the ingratitude and inconstancy of his countrymen, he persuaded himself that they still needed (and really wanted) his stabilizing leadership.

Much more serious, and more unexpected, was the second episode: the crisis of May 1968 (for which the French prefer the euphemism *"les événements"*—simply "the events"). On January 1, in his annual lecture mislabeled a press conference, de Gaulle had spoken somewhat smugly of France as a stable and secure island in a world of dissension and disorder. Like most of his countrymen, he had no sense of an impending domestic crisis. Unlike most of them, he failed to take that crisis seriously when it came in May, and waited until it was almost too late to recoup; even in retrospect he was to remain baffled, describing the upheaval (in his memoirs) as "incomprehensible." May 1968 was not to be his finest hour, even though he triumphed in the end.

"The events" began modestly, as a culmination of months of student unrest in universities in and near Paris. A series of discontents coalesced to produce the explosion: overcrowding and outmoded methods in the universities, gloomy job prospects for graduates, factional battles pitting students of the far left against those of the far right. The government's mishandling of the situation allowed these campus disruptions to mushroom into a full-scale confrontation in the Latin Quarter between student rebels and the forces of order: barricades went up in the streets, riot police were called in, the Sorbonne area became a kind of war zone. De Gaulle refused to be diverted from a planned journey to Rumania; he set off to mend French fences in the Balkans. When he returned, the Latin Quarter had been evacuated by the police and was in the hands of the student rebels; they had occupied the vast Sorbonne building and had turned it into the world's largest commune.

In a fury, de Gaulle demanded that his ministers recall the riot police to reconquer the Sorbonne. For once the ministers demurred, fearing that action would create martyrs and preferring to play for time. But the crisis only got worse; strikes began to break out spontaneously in factories around the country and merged into a general strike that idled some ten million workers. A kind of creeping paralysis set in: public services were interrupted, "action committees" took over everywhere, the entire system slowly ground to a halt. De Gaulle was provoked to act at last. He went on television to appeal for order and to propose some mild reforms. The speech was a disaster; viewers got the impression not of a savior but of a querulous old man, verging perhaps on senility. In the days that followed, the president vanished from public attention while Prime Minister Georges Pompidou shouldered the task of trying to persuade the strikers to go back to work. The presidential palace, the Elysée, seemed a kind of mausoleum, housing a moribund head of state; it was ignored by the rioters.

But, at the very moment when his regime and his career seemed finished, de Gaulle worked his own resurrection. It was sheer political theater: on May 29 he suddenly canceled a cabinet meeting without explanation, flew off by helicopter to an unknown destination, and simply vanished from sight. It was widely believed that he had gone to Colombey and would announce his resignation shortly. That, however, was not his plan. He returned to Paris the next day in the same whirlwind fashion, and let it be known that the French army commanders stationed in Germany were ready to move if needed to quell disorder. In a fighting speech by radio—perhaps the most remarkable four-minute speech since the Gettysburg address—he dissolved parliament, ordered new elections, and called on all patriotic Frenchmen to choose between the two alternatives before them: de Gaulle and anarchy. His supporters, demor-

Photo: Roger-Viollet.

alized until now, were buoyed by new hope: they filled the Champs-Elysées within an hour and roared about in flag-waving cars through most of the night. By the next day the crisis was over, except for clearing the Sorbonne of its squatter occupants; the strikers returned to work, Parisians took off for the beach or the country for a long weekend (followed, on their return, by the biggest traffic jam in European history), and everyone turned to the election campaign and to clearing away the accumulated garbage.

Once again, it seemed, de Gaulle had proved his mastery, his capacity to sense the right psychological moment for action, his knack for finding the right phrases to arouse his followers. Yet the May crisis was costly to his prestige and weighed on his spirits. He had recouped his fortunes, but only at the last possible moment, and after having lost control of events to a disastrous degree. Prime Minister Pompidou had quite obviously borne up better than de Gaulle during the crisis and was beginning to act like a prospective successor to the throne. It was Pompidou who led the Gaullist forces in the electoral campaign in June and who got the credit for scoring the most overwhelming victory the Gaullist party would ever win. With order restored and the opposition crushed, de Gaulle moved promptly to reassert his own primacy: he dismissed Pompidou and substituted a more pliable follower, Maurice Couve de Murville, explaining unconvincingly that Pompidou was being reserved for higher duties in the future. The country slowly slid back toward normalcy. De Gaulle, after all, still had four years of his term to serve, and parliament now was little more than a Gaullist club.

Then came de Gaulle's incomprehensible move: in 1969 he proposed two relatively minor constitutional reforms, and called on the nation to ratify them by referendum. The opponents of both reforms joined forces, and all the discontented groups that were still smarting from their defeat in 1968 seized their opportunity. The president was impelled to throw his personal weight onto the scales. If the referendum failed, he announced, he would draw the appropriate conclusions and would resign from office. Did he foresee the outcome, and prepare for it in advance? There were many who believed after the fact that he must have anticipated defeat, perhaps even from the very start. Indeed, some argued that since de Gaulle was far too shrewd to miscalculate so badly, he must have engineered the whole thing to provide himself with an excuse for dramatically abandoning power rather than dragging out the last years of his term in unglamorous fashion. Far more likely, however, is the hypothesis that since May 1968 his damaged prestige had gnawed on his spirits and had driven him to prove, via a referendum pitting himself against all his critics, that the mystical link between President de Gaulle and the nation was as strong as ever. Even great men can make mistakes; this seems to have been a blunder so big that only a big man could have made it.

His defeat in the referendum (by a fifty-three to forty-seven margin) was followed by a typical Gaullist response: he did not announce a formal resignation but simply abdicated, withdrawing into total silence and obscurity. He issued no statement, spoke no word of support for or criticism of his successors, made no public appearances, received almost no visitors as he holed up at Colombey-les-Deux-Eglises. He plunged once more into the second round of his memoirs, suspended since the 1950s; the initial volume, focused on the war in Algeria, appeared in October 1970 and sold out (one hundred thousand copies) the first day. Then, a month later, as he sat over an evening game of solitaire while his wife read at his side, came the sudden stroke that felled him like a giant oak.

The public response, throughout the world as well as in France, was overwhelming. Everyone rushed to pay him tribute—even those who had been his irreconcilable critics or had suffered under his lofty disapproval. And almost everyone spoke of him in terms of his role in history—which suggested, perhaps, that he was at least partly right in saying once that every Frenchman was Gaullist at heart. "In the short run," he had told a disciple, "events may seem to prove me wrong, but History will prove me right."

History, unfortunately, never *proves* anyone right or wrong; not even historians manage to do that, even though they try. Still, it seems safe to say that future histories are not likely to credit him with a lasting renovation of France's institutional structure on a Napoleonic scale, though his creation of a stronger and more stable executive power *may* survive. Nor will they credit him with some new conception or dream such as a united Europe or a transformed and more humane society. If future generations do read about de Gaulle—as surely they will—it is likely to be on account of the sheer dramatic impact of the man, the role he played in a time of upheaval, the striking pattern of withdrawal and return. The historical record does not provide us with many giants who cast long shadows for posterity. De Gaulle seems destined to be one of those, even though he may have been more a man of the past than of the future.

The American journalist James Reston, seeking a proper tribute at the end of de Gaulle's career, turned back to the little-known British poet of the nineteenth century, Stephen Phillips, who must have anticipated someone of de Gaulle's stature:

> O for a living man to lead
> Who will not babble when we bleed;
> O for the silent doer of the deed!
>
> One that is happy in his height,
> And one that in a nation's night
> Hath solitary certitude of light.

EPILOGUE

"IF IT BE TRUE THAT 'good wine needs no bush,' 'tis true that a good play needs no epilogue"; so affirmed Shakespeare, at the close of his play *As You Like It*. ("Bush," for those whose Elizabethan English may be a little rusty, was the Shakespearean equivalent of "commercial plug" or "hype.") Shakespeare's stricture should also apply, I suspect, in the case of a book. Epilogues are intended to recapitulate, to pull things together, to make sure that the inattentive reader understands What It Was All About; and one supposes that if a book's theme is clear, the writing cogent, and the reader alert, there will be no need for recapitulation. Nevertheless, custom dictates some sort of concluding remarks, and perhaps a conclusion is especially called for in a book made up of a series of loosely connected vignettes whose most obvious links are chronological sequence and a common Frenchness. Some readers may be reminded of Winston Churchill's remark after skeptically tasting an unfamiliar dessert: "This pudding has no theme."

Still, is it essential that every book be bound tightly together by a single all-pervasive theme? The answer depends, I suspect, on one's general world view. Some years ago the Oxford philosopher Sir Isaiah Berlin published a charming and provocative essay entitled "The Hedgehog and the Fox"; his title was drawn from a line of ancient Greek poetry that reads: "The fox knows many things, but the hedgehog knows one big thing." Most writers, thinkers, human beings, Sir Isaiah suggested, are either hedgehogs or foxes in their views of man and the universe. The hedgehog insists on relating everything to a single central vision, a universal organizing principle from which all significance derives. The fox's system of thought is "scattered or diffused, moving on many levels, seizing upon the essence of a vast variety of experiences and objects for what they are in themselves, without . . . seeking to fit them into . . . one unitary inner vision." Plato, Pascal, Hegel, Marx, Dostoevsky, Nietzsche were hedgehogs; Aristotle, Montaigne, Shakespeare, Molière, Goethe, Balzac were foxes.

It was not Sir Isaiah's purpose to take sides in this confrontation of human types; his scheme was merely a heuristic device for greater clarity and understanding. I suspect, however, that he leans toward the foxes, as I certainly do myself. The sketches contained in *Insiders and Outliers* do not illustrate any overarching theme, do not preach one gospel or convey one message. Each chapter has its own theme; each character in this procession of Frenchmen plays his own peculiar role in history. If anything binds them together (beyond that essential trait of common humanity that all of us share), it is their uniqueness as individuals, their resistance to treatment as faceless blobs on the screen of history or as mere statistical units like experimental fruit flies.

Most of these men did not change the course of events very much, if at all; all of them were products of their time and place, and their actions (so far as we can ever detect the springs of human actions) were not the outgrowth of purely autonomous choice but were in considerable part determined by natural or social forces. Yet these men made some choices too, and at times their choices did make a difference—at least for themselves and for a good number of their compatriots. And even when the significance of their actions was slight, something of permanence remains. "History," the Cambridge historian Herbert Butterfield once said, "is an intricate network formed by all the things that happen to individuals—and all the things that individuals do." It is more than that, of course; it is also the analysis of structure and process—of change and continuity over time. Yet, as Butterfield insists, "the genius of historical events lies in human beings." And the lives and deeds of both insiders and outliers remain an integral part of the rich and varied pattern of the past—that crowded, cluttered, often chaotic pattern that we call human history.

READER'S GUIDE

SIR ALAN BULLOCK'S provocative lecture at Cambridge, from which I have quoted in introducing this gallery of portraits, is well worth reading in its entirety; it puts in masterly fashion the case for the old-fashioned view of the individual's role in history. The lecture has been published in pamphlet form by the Cambridge University Press: *Is History Becoming a Social Science? The Case of Contemporary History* (1977). A classic statement of the opposite point of view appears in the conclusion of Fernand Braudel's *The Mediterranean and the Mediterranean World in the Age of Philip II* (translated by Sian Reynolds, New York: Harper & Row, 1976).

Chapter 1

Serious studies of Ouvrard and Vidocq are rare. The two best books on Ouvrard are Otto Wolff's *Ouvrard, Speculator of Genius* (translated by S. Thomson, New York: David McKay, 1962) and Maurice Payard's *Le financier G.-J. Ouvrard* (Reims: Académie Nationale de Reims, 1958). On Vidocq, Jean Savant's *La vie fabuleuse et authentique de Vidocq* (Paris: Seuil, 1950) is lively and detailed but rather uncritical. Vidocq's *Mémoires* have recently been reprinted in English translation: *Memoirs of Vidocq* (New York: Arno Press, 1976).

For an understanding of the Age of Balzac one cannot of course do better than to turn to Balzac's own novels: for example, *Père Goriot* (in which Vautrin first appears) and *Grandeurs et misères des courtisanes* (in which he plays a major role). *La maison Nucingen* focuses on that immigrant wheeler-dealer, the Baron de Nucingen, who is probably modeled after Roth-schild but who may be Balzac's composite of the high-flying financiers of his day.

Chapter 2

Lacenaire is another who has drawn little scholarly attention (and for obvious reasons; such deviants are not the scholar's business!). His memoirs were reprinted recently: *Mémoires de Lacenaire* (Paris: Michel, 1968), and Monique Marseille-Lansiart has done a brief impressionistic essay called *Lacenaire, assassin et poète* (Paris: Bourgoin, 1965). There is a long account of Lacenaire's life (identifying him as *"odieux assassin")* in the Larousse *Grand Dictionnaire Universel* of the mid-nineteenth century. The translated script of Marcel Carné's film *Children of Paradise* is also of some interest. On Pierre Rivière we have little beyond the collection of documents and essays produced by Michel Foucault and his students: *I, Pierre Rivière, Having Slaughtered my Mother, my Sister, and my Brother* . . . (translated by Frank Jellinek, New York: Pantheon, 1975).

Chapter 3

With Lamartine it's quite a different story; one could build a small library of books about him (though many of them focus on his literary side). Probably the most useful of the biographical studies are those by Jean Lucas-Dubreton, *Lamartine* (Paris: Flammarion, 1951) and Henri Guillemin, *Lamartine en 1848* (Paris: Presses Universitaires, 1948). Three notable figures were eyewitnesses to all or some of the events of 1848 in Paris and have left reminiscences that are well worth reading. Karl Marx's *The Class Struggles in France, 1848 to 1850,* an essay in instant history, was published in 1850 and has been frequently reprinted since then. Alexis de Tocqueville's *Recollections* has recently appeared in a new translation by George Lawrence (New York: Doubleday, 1970). And Gustave Flaubert's *A Sentimental Education* contains, in its later pages, a classic fictional account of the revolutionary era, seen by an unsympathetic observer.

Chapter 4

The best and most up-to-date biography of Clemenceau is by an English scholar: David R. Watson, *Georges Clemenceau* (London: Eyre Methuen, 1974). Also useful is a work by one of the Tiger's former disciples: Georges Wormser, *La République de Clemenceau* (Paris, Presses Universitaires, 1961). On Jaurès, there is a first-rate biography by Harvey Goldberg, *The Life of Jean Jaurès* (Madison: University of Wisconsin Press, 1962). Marcelle Auclair's *La vie de Jaurès* (Paris: Seuil, 1954) offers a more personal portrait.

Chapter 5

The only detailed account of Dr. Mans's heroic resistance career is that by "Remy" [Gilbert Renault-Roulier], *L'Opération Jericho* (Paris: France-Empire, 1954). On the René Hardy case, there is the published summation by his lawyer Maurice Garçon, *Plaidoyer pour René Hardy* (Paris: Fayard, 1950). Hardy's second trial was covered in great detail by the Paris daily *Le Monde* (April 22 to May 10, 1950). Hardy himself, after his acquittal, embarked on a new career as a novelist; one of his novels, *Le livre de la colère* (Paris: Laffont, 1951), draws heavily on his own experience. For the Oradour tragedy, there is a careful account by the Dane Jens Krusse: *Madness at Oradour* (translated by Carl Malmberg, London: Secker & Warburg, 1969). The role of the Alsatians in all this is analyzed by Henry Allainmat and Betty Truck in *La nuit des parias* (Paris: Presses de la Cité, 1974). *Life* magazine covered the trial and published some gripping pictures in the issue of February 23, 1953. On Pierre Laval, the most thorough and balanced study comes from the pen of English scholar Geoffrey Warner: *Pierre Laval and the Eclipse of France* (New York: Macmillan, 1969). My own attempt to weigh Laval's responsibilities and to compare them with Marshal Pétain's appeared in the *Virginia Quarterly Review*, Autumn 1958, under the title "Vichy Revisited."

Chapter 6

Charles de Gaulle, like Lamartine, has been much written about. He himself published five volumes of memoirs, which demonstrate his sense of his role in history and his attempt to influence its verdict. The most perceptive brief biography is that of Jean Lacouture: *De Gaulle* (translated by Francis K. Price, New York: New American Library, 1966). Jean Charlot's *The Gaullist Phenomenon* (London: Allen & Unwin, 1971) is an interesting assessment; and André Malraux's *Felled Oaks: Conversations with de Gaulle* (translated by Irene Clephane, New York: Holt, Rinehart, & Winston, 1971) sums up that great disciple's sentiments about his hero. John L. Hess's *The Case for de Gaulle* (New York: Morrow, 1968) is a good antidote for those Americans who believe de Gaulle to have been viciously anti-American. Finally, Stanley Hoffmann has some probing essays on de Gaulle and his times in his collection entitled *Decline or Renewal? France Since the 1930s* (New York: Viking, 1974).

ABOUT THE AUTHOR

"IN HIGH SCHOOL I WANTED to be either an archaeologist, hunting for petrified dinosaur eggs in the Gobi desert, or a Davis Cup tennis player," divulges Gordon Wright, one of the country's most eminent historians of France. "In college I first intended to become a chemical engineer, then a biologist, then a diplomat. In graduate school I set out to be a specialist on Germany, but found myself eventually facing a choice between Japan and France. So much for the well-planned career choice!"

Professor Wright is William H. Bonsall Professor of History, emeritus, at Stanford, where he received his M.A. (1935) and Ph.D. (1939) and has taught since 1957. He was executive head of Stanford's History Department from 1959 to 1965 and was associate dean of the School of Humanities and Sciences from 1970 to 1973. Though he is emeritus, he has continued to teach since retirement, at Stanford and at various universities around the country.

A native of Washington state, prior to coming to Stanford Gordon Wright taught for almost twenty years at the University of Oregon, with interruptions to serve as a visiting faculty member at Columbia and the National War College. During World War II, he spent a year as a State Department specialist on France and has twice since served as a foreign service officer in the U.S. Embassy in Paris—most recently as cultural attaché. He has been decorated by the French government with the Order of Arts and Letters.

Professor Wright was president of the American Historical Association in 1975. Also in that year he received the Lloyd W.

Dinkelspiel Award for outstanding service to undergraduate education. He is the author or editor of ten books on French and modern European history, including *The Ordeal of Total War, 1939–1945* and *France in Modern Times.* Professor Wright is a member of the American Academy of Arts and Sciences and the American Philosophical Society, and a corresponding member of the Académie des Sciences Morales et Politiques. He was awarded a Guggenheim Fellowship for 1980–81 and will be working in Paris on a history of evolving French attitudes toward what is generally known as "the crime problem."

Professor Wright lives on the Stanford campus with his wife, Louise Aiken Wright. They have four children: Eric, Michael, Philip, and David. Since bursitis wiped out tennis as his favorite recreation, he spends his spare time reading, listening to good music, watching Masterpiece Theatre, and fighting a rearguard action against Bermuda grass in his lawn.

CREDITS

PAGE xii   Henri Rousseau, *Myself: Portrait Landscape*. Courtesy National Gallery, Prague.

PAGE 6   Frontispiece from *Mémoires de Vidocq* (Paris: Librairie Charlieu Frères et Huillery, 1828).

PAGE 9   Canella, Guiseppe. Detail from a view of the Place de la Concorde in Balzac's time. Musée Carnavalet, Paris. Photo: Bulloz, Paris.

PAGE 14   Isabey, Louis-Gabriel-Eugène. *Madame Tallien*. Miniature. Bibliothèque Nationale, Paris.

PAGE 19   Villain, Henri Georges. *Gabriel Julien Ouvrard*. Lithograph from Ouvrard's *Memoirs*, vol. 11, 1827. Otto Wolff Collection. Bibliothèque Nationale, Paris.

PAGE 22   Vidocq, poacher turned gamekeeper, making an arrest. Préfecture de Police, Paris.

PAGE 28   Frontispiece from *Mémoires de Lacenaire*. Bibliothèque Nationale, Paris.

PAGE 33   Lacenaire in *Les Enfants du Paradis*, a film by Marcel Carné. Photo: The Museum of Modern Art/Film Stills Archive, New York.

PAGE 36   Lacenaire and his victim. Bibliothèque Nationale, Paris.

PAGE 40   Still from *Moi, Pierre Rivière, ayant égorgé ma mère, ma soeur et mon frère . . .* , a film by René Allio, from *Cahiers du Cinéma*, November 1976.

PAGE 42   Nadar. Portrait-caricature of Lamartine. Charcoal sketch on white gouache. Bibliothèque Nationale, Paris.

PAGE 47   Decainse, Louis-François. *Portrait de Lamartine*. 1839. Oil on canvas. Musée Municipal des Ursulines, Mâcon, France.

PAGE 52   Lamartine addressing the crowd at the Hôtel de Ville in 1848. *Illustrated London News*, April 22, 1848. Courtesy of the Stanford University Libraries, Stanford, California.

PAGE 60   *Rue St. Antoine, Souvenirs des Journées de Juin, 1848*. *Charivari*, August 18, 1848. Courtesy of the Stanford University Libraries Department of Special Collections, Stanford, California.

PAGE 62   *Le Jugement de Paris*, cartoon of the candidates for the 1848 election (Lamartine, second from right). *Charivari*, November 18, 1848. Courtesy of the Stanford University Libraries Department of Special Collections, Stanford, California.

PAGE 64   Manet, Edouard. *Clemenceau*. 1879. Oil on canvas. Musée du Louvre, Paris.

PAGE 71   Eloy-Vincent, A. Sketches of Jaurès as orator. 1910. Musée Jaurès de Castres, Castres, France.

PAGE 76   Caricature of Clemenceau. Photo: Collection, Roger-Viollet, Paris.

PAGE 83   Lloyd George, Orlando, Clemenceau, and Wilson at President Wilson's residence in Paris (from left to right). Photo: Collection, Roger-Viollet, Paris.

PAGE 86   Pierre Laval at his trial, October 1945. Photo: Keystone, London.

PAGE 101   Interior of the church at Oradour after the explosion and massacre, from *Oradour-sur-Glane: Vision d'Epouvante*. (Paris: Comité du Souvenir et de l'Association Nationale des Familles des Martyrs d'Oradour-sur-Glane, 1945.)

PAGE 103   Alsatian defendant in court at the Oradour massacre trial, 1953. Photo: Leonard McCombe. *Life* magazine, © 1953 Time Inc.

PAGE 106   Shepard, Ernest Howard. *The Juggler*. © 1940 Punch/Rothco.

PAGE 110   General Charles de Gaulle. Photo: Imperial War Museum, London.

PAGE 117   De Gaulle's grand descent on the Champs-Elysées, August 26, 1944. Photo: Keystone, London.

PAGE 120   De Gaulle in Algeria, June 1958: *"Je vous ai compris."* Photo: Keystone, London.

PAGE 125   De Gaulle with President John F. Kennedy. Photo: Sipa Press, Paris.

PAGE 130   De Gaulle during a press conference. Photo: Collection, Roger-Viollet, Paris.

PAGE 140   Gordon Wright. Photo: Courtesy of News and Publications Service, Stanford University, Stanford, California.

Index